Mountain Biking
Michigan

The Best Trails
In Northern
Lower Michigan

Other Books By Mike Terrell:

Northern Michigan's Best Cross Country Ski Trails

Mountain Biking
Michigan
The Best Trails
In Northern
Lower Michigan

By Mike Terrell

PUBLICATIONS

Published by Thunder Bay Press
Production and design by Pegg Legg Publications
Maps by Michelle Miller, Miller Design, Grand Rapids, MI
Printing by Eerdmans Printing Company, Grand Rapids, MI
Cover photo by Karen Gentry
Inside photography by Mike Terrell, Jim DuFresne and John Robert
Williams and Karen Gentry

ISBN: 1-882376-21-8

Printed in the United States of America

96 97 98 99 100   1 2 3 4 5 6 7 8

Holt, Michigan

Acknowledgment

I would like to acknowledge those who work hard to provide us with the many fine pathways we enjoy in this state...the many volunteers who help to maintain the trails, Department of Natural Resources personnel and U.S. Forest Service rangers. We owe them all a debt of gratitude for the many hours they put in developing and taking care of the many pathways we enjoy riding.

A special thanks to Jim DuFresne, noted outdoor writer and friend. It was his idea to come out with the two books really covering the Lower Peninsula, and it was his editing skills that brought them together.

And, last but certainly not least, a big thank you to my wife Kathy whose love and encouragement have helped to make this book possible. It takes a lot of hours away from home and family. A remarkable women who has been battling cancer since 1988, her "never give in" attitude has been inspirational to her family and friends. God bless you.

m.t.

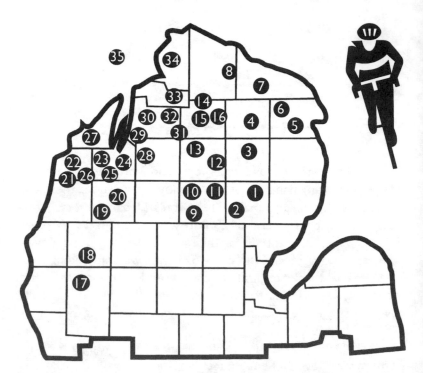

Mountain Biking Northern Michigan

Lake Huron
1. Rifle River
2. Omegaw Hills
3. Garland Resort
4. Buttles Road
5. Norway Ridge
6. Chippewa Hills
7. Ocqueoc Falls
8. Black Mountain

Highlands
9. Marl Lake
10. N. Higgins Lake
11. Tisdale Triangle

12. Wakeley Lake
13. Hartwick Pines
14. Green Timbers
15. High Country
16. Shingle Mill

Manistee Forest
17. Hungerford Lake
18. Pine Valleys
19. MacKenzie
20. Cadillac Pathway
21. Crystal Mountain
22. Betsie River

Grand Traverse
23. Muncie Lakes

24. Sand Lakes
25. Lost Lake
26. Lake Ann
27. Sugar Loaf
28. VASA
29. Grand Traverse
30. NORBA

Tip of the Mitt
31. Pine Baron
32. Warner Creek
33. Boyne Mountain
34. Wildwood Hills
35. Beaver Island

Contents

Manistee National Forest

Grand Traverse

Tip of the Mitt

North Country Trail

Other Trails

Mountain bikers race along the famous NORBA Trail at Schuss Mountain Resort in Antrim County. Although the NORBA is Michigan's largest race, the trail can be enjoyed throughout the summer and fall.

Mountain Biking Northern Michigan

The first time I tried mountain biking was on a sandy two-track near my home town of Traverse City. It felt like riding horizontal on a sand dune. I was not impressed.

That was 1982. My wife, Kathy, had talked me into trying it. I was an avid road rider, and a friend had told her how great it was. She was sure I would like it. She was right, and I was wrong.

It was on my third or fourth ride that I really became an advocate of the sport. I tried biking a nearby ski trail, the Sand Lakes Quiet Area, that is a popular mountain biking trail in the summer. It's mostly firm single-track, and I was hooked. It was all the things I enjoyed about cross country skiing; the solitude and beauty of pristine woodland settings, but at a pace that allowed me to enjoy much more of the trail system than if hiking.

At about the same time the sport started growing by leaps and bounds. Of course, I'm sure you're aware that mountain bikes today account for about 90 percent of all bike sales. Road biking still draws good crowds for organized rides, but mountain biking has captured the masses.

A weekend of National Off Road Biking Association (NORBA) competition at Shanty Creek draws close to 30,000 spectators and 1,500 participants. Michigan Mountain Biking Association (MMBA) competition around the state is drawing record numbers, as well as membership in the organization. The Iceman, which usually lives up to its name, is held annually the first Saturday in November, and draws 1500 frozen riders. More and more riders are demanding more and more space in our state and national forests.

The events are just the tip of the iceberg. They demonstrate the growing popularity of the sport, but the real demand is for everyday use by "citizen" riders...the non-racing type.

It's with this demand in mind that we've written what I believe to be the definitive books on mountain biking in the state. Between this book and it's companion book on the southern half of the Lower Peninsula, you have close to 90 good trails to choose from and many excellent single-track rides.

Rules of the Trail

We all enjoy the use of the land for our recreational pursuits such as mountain biking. With such usage comes responsibility. Mountain biking does impact the land and the trails we ride. Riding off the trail kills plants, and skidding your tires on steep inclines will cause erosion that will eventually rut the trail. Learn and practice sound environmental practices while riding.

"Leave no trace," and "pack-in, pack-out" are more than catchy phrases. You demonstrate your respect for the land in the way you ride. Ride in a way that will minimize your impact on the environment.

The International Mountain Bicycling Association has come up with six "Rules of the Trail" that all bikers should remember and follow:

1. Ride on open trails only. Respect trail and road closures, private property, and requirements for permits and authorization. Federal and state wilderness areas are closed to cycling, and some park and forest trails are also off limits.

2. Leave no trace. Don't ride when the ground will be marred, such as on certain soils after a rain. Never ride off the trail, skid your tires, or discard any object. Strive to pack out more than you pack in.

3. Control your bicycle. Inattention for even a second can cause disaster. Excessive speed frightens and injures people, gives mountain biking a bad name, and results in trail closures.

4. Always yield the trail. Make your approach known well in advance. A friendly greeting is considerate and appreciated. Show your respect when passing others by slowing to walking speed or even stopping. Anticipate that other trail users may be around corners or in blind spots.

5. Never spook animals.

6. Plan ahead. Know your equipment, your ability, and the area in which you are riding and prepare accordingly.
Be self-sufficient at all times, keep your bike in good repair, and carry necessary supplies for changes in weather. Keep trails open by setting an example of responsible cycling for all to see.

The Michigan Mountain Biking Association also has a Responsibility Code:

1. *Always yield the right of way to other trail users*
2. *Slow down and pass with care (or stop)*
3. *Control your speed at all times*
4. *Stay on designated trails*
5. *Don't disturb wildlife or livestock*
6. *Pack out litter*
7. *Respect public and private property*
8. *Know local rules*
9. *Plan ahead*
10. *Minimize impact*
11. *Avoid riding in large groups*
12. *Report incidents of trail impasse to local authorities.*

When To Ride

Although there isn't a rule of thumb, don't start riding before the frost has had chance to leave the ground. In northern Michigan that can occur anywhere from mid-March to mid-April, depending on the severity of the winter. On the other end, you can normally ride up to firearm deer season, which starts November 15. Once the 16-day season begins, remember that bullets and bikers don't mix well. It's rare that you can bike after the deer season in northern Michigan until the following spring.

The snowfall is long and deep in the winter. I can only recall a couple of Decembers in 17 winters of living up here that have been dry enough to permit mountain biking. January, February and March have never been good for riding. April is marginal and even May is sometimes dicey because of cold, damp weather. June, July, August, September and October are the best months for planning a mountain biking trip in northern Michigan. Any other time of the year, and it's a "role of the dice."

Trail Fees

Hopefully some day the state of Michigan will be collecting trail fees in the form of an annual pass from mountain bikers, much like the system currently in place for snowmobilers. It's long overdue.

A trail users fee has been in effect for years in such states as Wisconsin and Minnesota and it works well for them. The few state trails in Michigan that are groomed for cross country skiing have been through the efforts of volunteer groups. Much of the trail maintenance over the last few years for mountain biking has been largely due to volunteer efforts from MMBA Chapters throughout the state as well as other groups.

The donation pipes located at many trailheads around the state aren't working. It's a shame, but users have not been willing to support the trail systems through donations and it's time to "pay the piper." You can't bike or ski on pathways littered with fallen trees and limbs. When signs have disappeared from critical inter-sections, they have not been replaced, creating a potentially dangerous situation for those who don't know the trail. The time has come for us to pay our way. If we don't, I think you'll see several system closed in the next few years. We already have designated areas that are unusable, and with the increased usage of all our

Mountain biking can be a great family activity with the right training.

forest pathways in the last few years, we need more, not less.

If the permit fee is implemented, it will most likely be administered through the computer system already in place to sell fishing and hunting licenses. Between DNR offices, bike shops and resorts operating near state trails, finding the permit shouldn't be difficult.

Until an annual trail fee is put in place, please use the donation

Trail Difficulty

The Trail Difficulty rating used in this book was a way to indicate the physical exertion required to ride the route. It's influenced by the elevation gain (length and steepness) and technical difficulty of a ride including, width and character of the trail, obstacles (roots, sand, etc.), and length of technical sections.

Easy: This is a flat, no-brainer ride with very little elevation gain along a fairly wide trail or possibly a two-track.

Moderate: These trails will include some elevation change and often short technical sections. They require more endurance than technical skills and can usually be handled by beginners who are prepared to hop off their bike from time to time.

Strenuous: These routes will include some long, big hills that may require getting off your bike up if you fail to change gears soon enough. It could mean long stretches of narrow single track where technical expertise is required to dodge rocks or hop over roots.

Some bikers will tell you that anybody can do any trail as long as they are prepared to hop off their bike and walk when the going gets too tough. That's debatable. But there is no shame and for many it's a lot safer to walk the technical segments of a strenuous trail. It will also open up a lot more terrain for you as even the hardest trails have numerous easy sections to enjoy.

The important thing is to try and figure out your time and pace to let others know when and where you will finish. You should always let someone know where you're going and when you'll be back, especially if you ride alone.

The Future Of Mountain Biking

Michigan is at the forefront of mountain biking in the Midwest. With the presence and political help of the MMBA, we have several fine single-track trails established throughout the state. However, despite the success the sport has enjoyed, there is reason for concern regarding the future.

There's a lot of competition for state and federal land

use...hikers, bikers, cross country skiers, snowmobilers, equestrians, hunters and off-road vehicle users. Not all of these uses are compatible and conflicts are inevitable.

We, as mountain bikers, can do a lot to avoid user conflicts on the trails we use. Ride under control at all times. You never know when you may encounter other trail users. Personally, when hikers are encountered along the trail, I like to get off my bike, walk around them and take the time to chat with them.

That is the single biggest complaint among hikers that were surveyed by US Forest Service personnel along the North Country Trail (NCT). They claim bikers "blow by," forcing them off the trail without so much as an "excuse me." That's not the way to win friends or influence anyone.

Another way to create a positive image is by helping to maintain the trails we ride. That is being done, especially in the southern half the state where MMBA chapters have sprung up around trails to help maintain them. The Northern Michigan chapter has taken on portions of the NCT for maintenance, bridging and stabilization.

In the northern Lower Peninsula, the Mason Tract and Jordan River Pathways have been closed to mountain bikes. Other pathways are under study by the Michigan Department of Natural Resources and U.S. Forest Service...especially the NCT, which offers many excellent single-track rides. Unfortunately, politics are often the real reason, when catch-all phrases like "environmental and safety concerns" are used.

I encourage you to get involved with the MMBA, help to maintain the trails you enjoy riding, and remember why you took up mountain biking in the first place.

The peace, beauty and solitude of our woodland areas is sacred to all of us. Go forth quietly, ride under control at all times and leave as little trace of your passing as possible. And, most important of all, be friendly and courteous to other trail users. Don't take your right to ride in the woods for granted.

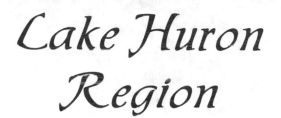

Lake Huron Region

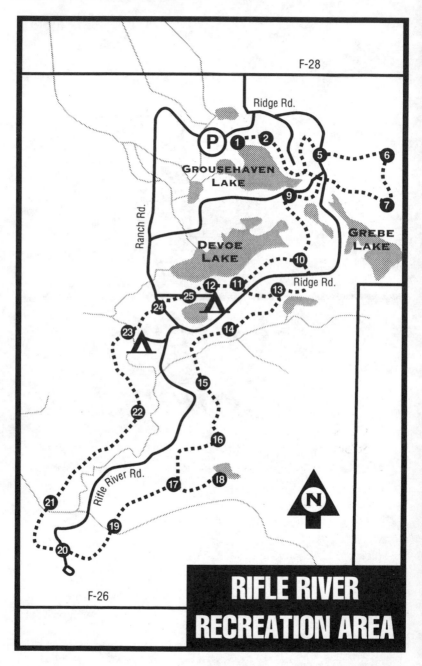

RIFLE RIVER
RECREATION AREA

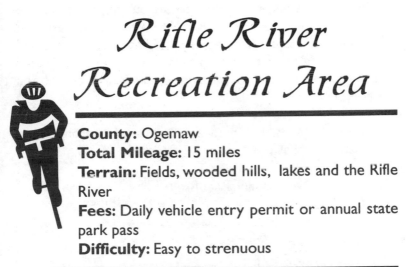

Rifle River
Recreation Area

County: Ogemaw
Total Mileage: 15 miles
Terrain: Fields, wooded hills, lakes and the Rifle River
Fees: Daily vehicle entry permit or annual state park pass
Difficulty: Easy to strenuous

The Rifle River Recreation Area has some of the most scenic mountain biking trails in the Lower Peninsula. The firm, single-track trail meanders over the hills ringing the 10 lakes located within the park as well as cuts through the thick forests of the river bottoms. It flows along the banks of the swift Rifle River and glides through beautiful, open grasslands.

At times the riding is easy, and other times extremely difficult. The two distinct halves can be biked separately or in tandem. The total length of the entire trail is about 15 miles. If you elect to ride just the easy, mostly flat river bottoms, the distance is roughly 10 miles. Or, if you want to ride just the more difficult hills in the lake section, there's a 7.5 mile loop.

In this 4,329-acre state park unit, you have all kind of choices as a mountain biker.

The trail system is well marked with numbered posts keyed to the map. Take a map with you on the ride. It can be confusing without one as there are places where trails merge with other trails and roads.

The preserve was formerly a private hunting and fishing retreat and became a state park unit in 1963. With numerous campsites from which to choose, campers will find campgrounds with modern sites (electric hookups and showers) to rustic. In addition, there are five rustic cabins with six bunk beds in each that are available for rent.

Getting There: The park entrance is located on County Road F-28, 4.5 miles due east of Rose City and M-33.

Information: Contact Rifle River Recreation Area, 2550 E. Rose City Rd, Lupton, MI 48635; ☎ (517) 437-2258.

Rifle River Recreation Area

Distance: 12 miles
Trail: Single track and forest road
Direction: Clockwise

The trailhead actually starts on the east side of the Grousehaven Lake Campground. I like to start at the picnic shelter also located on Grousehaven. It cuts about a mile off the ride, but more importantly, it's less crowded. I don't like bothering the campers.

Post 4 is found at the back of the parking lot near the picnic shelter. The trail quickly climbs a small ridge, and takes off to the left. Within a short distance, the trail forks. Take the left branch over to Post 5. After crossing the road, the trail rolls up and down some big, heavily forested hills for the next 1.5 miles. This section is a real roller-coaster ride. Watch for sand and roots on the turns of the downhill sections. It can be rough at times. The long, downhill run to Post 8 is a blast.

After, again crossing the main park road, take a secondary

A bridge on the trail system in Rifle River Recreation Area.

road to the left from Post 8, reached at **Mile 1.7**. It immediately plunges down to the narrow strip of land between Lodge and Grousehaven Lakes. It's a beautiful spot to linger and enjoy the serenity of the area. Continue following the dirt road up the hill. Within a short distance the trail again takes off as a single track to the left.

The 0.7-mile section between Posts 9 and 10 plunges up and down a ridge line offering some pretty views and some killer hills. Shortly after crossing a low, wet area the trail climbs two steep sections. The crest of the second hill affords a nice view of Lodge Lake on the left and Devoe Lake with all of its islands on the right.

Enjoy the view, because quickly coming up is the toughest climb on the ride, a real thigh-burner. A quick downhill run takes you by a pretty, little pond with a couple of large, active beaver lodges.

After reaching Post 10 at **Mile 2.5**, the rest of the ride tames down. Take the left fork at the post and continue across Ridge Road, a dirt road, and through the open grasslands around Scaup Lake to Post 13. This is where the river bottom section of the ride begins.

To do just the easy portion of the ride, park at the campgrounds on Devoe Lake. Post 12 is on the north side of the parking lot and from there you follow the trail up to Post 11 and then right to Post 13, a ride of less than a mile.

The trail continues along and then crosses Skunk Creek at **Mile 4**. You see lots of beaver activity in this area. It's also a good place to spot eagles. The trail is a little rough in spots because of the roots, but rideable. At times the canopy of trees is so thick, it can be dark on a sunny day.

It's best to avoid the short spur over to Post 18 at Lost Lake. The trail is usually wet while this small lake is a very sensitive bog area that can be easily damaged by the fat tires of a mountain bike.

At **Mile 7** or 3 miles after crossing Skunk Creek you cross a suspension bridge over the Rifle River to Post 20 on the south side. Be prepared to walk your bike across this foot bridge. For the next mile the trail meanders in and out of thick forests and along the banks of the scenic river. Shortly before reaching Post 22 at **Mile 8.4**, the landscape changes to open grasslands.

After crossing the river again at Post 23, the trail merges with the Devoe Lake campground road and ends at Post 25 at **Mile 9.6**. Follow the campground road to Post 12 and continue to Post 11. Take the left fork to Post 10 at **Mile 10.6** and retrace your tracks to Post 8, if you want to follow the trail.

I like to swing over and follow Ridge Road from post 10 over to Post 8. In little over a half mile it climbs over a ridge between Lodge and Grebe Lake. Take the time to climb the observation tower. It offers incredible vistas of the entire park and several of the lakes.

In less than a half mile after the tower, you reach the point where the trail again crosses the road, turn left to Post 8. Continue on across the dirt road, and in a third of a mile you'll be back at the parking lot.

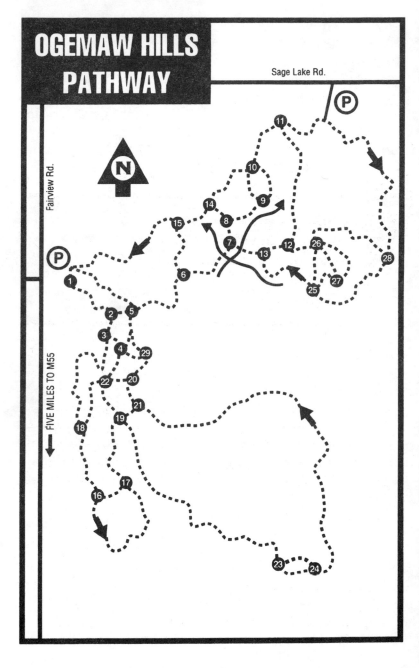

OGEMAW HILLS PATHWAY

Sage Lake Rd.

Fairview Rd.

FIVE MILES TO M55

Ogemaw Hills

County: Ogemaw
Total Mileage: 13.6 miles
Terrain: Rolling, wooded upland area
Fees: Donation
Difficulty: Easy to strenuous

West Branch may look a little flat as you zip past it along I-75 but just a few miles north of the town is a hilly, even rugged area that has been a long-time favorite for cross country skiers and in recent years has attracted the attention of mountain bikers.

The result of extensive glacier activity, this ridge of hills, site of the Ogemaw Hills Pathway, is known as the West Branch Moraine. The ridgeline arcs to the south for many miles and was formed 16,000 years ago by a retreating glacier known as the Saginaw lobe.

The 13.6-mile trail system was developed by a number of local organizations including the Ogemaw Ski Council and the West Branch Kiwanis and Optimist Clubs. There are a dozen loops that make up the system and range in difficulty from easy to strenuous with the vast majority rated moderate for mountain bikers.

With 28 signposts scattered around the

system you'll need a map to follow. It's an imaginative system offering all kinds of options. The ride described here follows the outer parameter, but at any point (with a map) you can shorten or extend the ride. Each trail segment is marked for one-way travel.

Getting There: Take the I-75 business loop through West Branch to Fairview Road and head north for about five miles. The trailhead parking is located on the right.

Information: Contact the Roscommon DNR Regional Office, P.O. Box 218, Roscommon, MI 48653; ☎ (517) 275-5151.

Ogemaw Hills Pathway

Distance: 11 miles
Trail: Single track
Direction: Counter clockwise

From the trailhead, ride east to Post 2. The firm, single-track trail swings south for the next mile as it rolls through deep woods by Post 3 to Post 18 and Post 16. (I told you it gets confusing without a map). For the next half mile, the trail drops down a small ridge and then ascends to Post 17. From there it's an easy ride over to Post 19, reached at *Mile 2.3*.

The next couple of segments total 3 miles as the trail swings out to an overlook and back. This is an interesting segment, arguably the gem of the system. It rolls through a combination of hardwoods and pines and by cedar swamps. The few cleared areas you border were once old homesteads, slowly being reclaimed by the land. You can still see the rock fence lines if you look closely.

Post 23 is reached at *Mile 3.3*, where you intersect the overlook spur to the right, which is definitely worth the short trip. Located on the face of the West Branch Moraine, the overlook provides a striking view of what took place here centuries ago. You can see how the land stretching out in front of you, now dotted with farms, could have contained a great inland lake and today still resembles a great basin. With a bench located here, it's a great spot on a sunny day to relax and enjoy the view.

As you leave the overlook, the trail proceeds to drop sharply down a steep, sandy slope, swings back to the left at the bottom and then starts a long strenuous climb. It's the only long, grueling climb you have through the first six or seven miles of the ride. That's followed by a nice half-mile gentle downhill run while the rest of the ride to Post 21, reached at **Mile 5.3**, rolls up and down some small hills.

The next stretch through Posts 20 to 29 is an easy half mile and then you have a choice. A right takes you through a steep little valley and is more difficult. A left to Post 4 and then a right to Post 5 is much easier, and only slightly longer. Post 5 is reached at **Mile 6** and a left here takes you back to the parking lot.

Continuing on the long ride the trail rolls for a mile through Posts 6 and 7 and over to Post 8. The trail drops slightly as you take a right to Post 9. Again you have a choice of easy or more difficult for the short ride to Post 10. The trail climbs slightly as it heads to Post 11, reached at **Mile 7.5**.

The next 2.5 miles is the tough part of the ride. As you leave Post 11 the trail drops down into a deep, little valley and then quickly climbs out. Shortly after you pass the spur that leads over to a second trailhead off Sage Lake Road, the trail begins a long drop to Post 28. Reached at **Mile 8.8**, this is one of the longest downhill runs in the Lower Peninsula. It's not steep, but it's easy to gain speed. Watch for the hard right turn at the bottom.

The trail climbs back out of the valley as you proceed through Post 25 back to Post 13. If you want more hills and thrills, take a right at Post 25, climb to Post 26, plunge down to Post 27, climb back to Post 26 and take a right for a fast, thrilling ride back down to Post 28. It's about a mile of steep up and down trail.

At Post 13, head left back to Post 7, over to Post 8, and left again for a short ride to Post 14, reached at **Mile 10.2**. It's less than a mile and an easy ride back to the parking lot as the trail rolls through Post 15 and back to the trailhead. The open areas you pass through on the ride back are remnants of old farms.

29

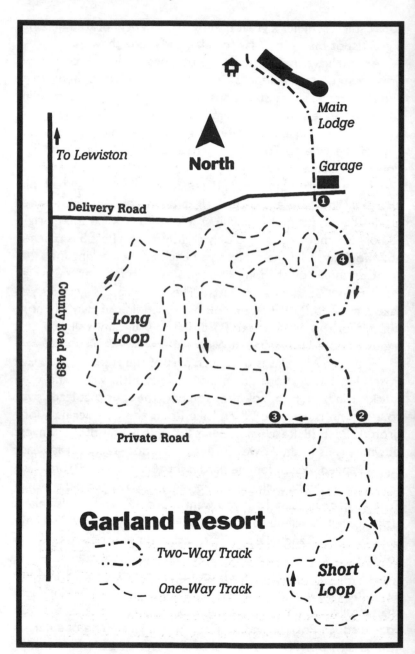

To Lewiston

North

Main Lodge

Garage

Delivery Road

County Road 489

Long Loop

Private Road

Garland Resort

Two-Way Track

One-Way Track

Short Loop

Garland Resort

County: Oscoda
Total Mileage: 5 miles
Terrain: Rolling forested hills with some good climbs
Fees: A trail fee is paid at the Pro Shop.
Difficulty: Easy to strenuous

Garland is best known as a Nordic ski resort in the winter and one of the premier golf destinations in the Lower Peninsula in the summer with four beautiful 18-hole courses. The centerpiece of the resort village is a massive log lodge, said to be the largest east of the Mississippi River. The lodging surrounding the main lodge is exquisite. Many of the rooms and condos feature fireplaces and European-style four-poster beds. The noted Herman's Restaurant offers a wide selection of wonderful and unusual gourmet dishes...many featuring local wild game.

The resort also includes an indoor pool, an outdoor hot tub and as of 1995 mountain biking. Utilizing the resort's ski trails, this new system makes for a short, easy but pleasant ride in the woods. The entire route is a 5-mile ride or, by utilizing a double track at the beginning, can be shortened to a 3-mile outing.

What Garland lacks in mileage, can easily be supplemented by riding other nearby trail systems; Buttles Road, Hartwick Pines and Wakeley Lake are all within a half-hour. There are also numerous dirt roads and two-tracks in the Mackinaw State Forest that surrounds Lewiston while two other resorts nearby, Lakeview Hills Resort (☎ 517-786-2000) and Pine Ridge Lodge (☎ 517-786-4789), each has their own trail system for bikers.

Getting There: The resort is located on CR-489 5 miles south of Lewiston and 12 miles north of Luzerne.

Information: For reservations or additional information call Garland at ☎ (800) 968-0042.

Long Trail

Distance: 5 miles
Trail: Single and double track
Direction: Clockwise

The ride begins in front of the main lodge and heads south. Follow the paved pathway to Post 1, which is just on the other side of the Delivery Road by the maintenance garage. It's just a short ride over to Post 4 on a double track trail. Continue straight ahead as the trail entering from the right is the return trail.

At this point the trail winds along the edge of the golf course, but well back in the woods. Just before *Mile 1*, you reach Post 2 at the edge of a private dirt road. Cross the road to the single track on the south side. For the next 1.2 miles the trail gently winds through wooded, rolling hills. It's easy riding, and frequently a great place to spot deer.

Post 3 is reached at *Mile 2.2* and you have the option of turning right on the private road and return to the lodge, via the two-way track, for a 3-mile ride. To continue on the Long Trail and the harder portion of this ride, head left on the dirt road and pick up the trail where it resumes in the woods.

Best known as a cross country ski resort, Garland also has a trail system for mountain bikers as well as bike rentals for overnight guests.

This portion was laid out as a ski trail by U.S. Ski Hall of Fame nominee Vojin Baic. The resort wanted to add some bite to their otherwise mostly flat, easy trail system. He succeeded.

The trail curls up and down the ridge three times in the next 1.5 miles. The downhill runs are fast and pretty straight forward, but watch for a hard left turn at the bottom of the first long downhill. After negotiating the turn, the trail meanders through a nice section of woods before beginning the second long climb. The downhill run is two tiered, which makes it kind of exciting. You can't see what's over the second tier as you plunge down the first drop. It's a straight descent that will cause few problems for most bikers, but it still gets the adrenaline flowing.

Immediately after reaching the bottom you circle back and begin a third climb up the ridge. This is the one that really leaves me gasping for air. It's the longest, hardest climb of the three, and seems to go on forever.

Once on top, the trail flows along the ridge for about a mile, meandering quickly up and down the flank in little dips...no more long, long climbs, just short ones. Shortly before reaching Post 4, you take one more plunge down the flank and back up but it's neither as long or as tiring as the first three. The trail eventually descends to Post 4, where you can then head back to the lodge for some libations at Herman's.

Buttles Road Pathway

County: Montmorency
Total Mileage: 6 miles
Terrain: Sinkhole valleys, lightly wooded hills and lots of open areas
Fees: None
Difficulty: Easy

Buttles Road Pathway is a pretty little system that's definitely worth exploring if you're staying at Garland or nearby Gaylord. It's an easy riding system with only one good hill on the backside of Loop C near Crystal Lake. The trail rims a couple of long sinkhole valleys rolling through Jack pine forests, and over open meadows.

The entire system is a 6-mile ride and highly recommended as the most scenic sections are along Loop C, but shorter loops of 1.75 miles and 3 miles can also be followed. The only drawback of the Buttles Road Pathway is the natural gas and oil drilling activity that takes place here.

Getting There: The trailhead parking lot is located 3 miles south of M-32 on Buttles Road and 9 miles east of Johannesburg. Lewiston is

35

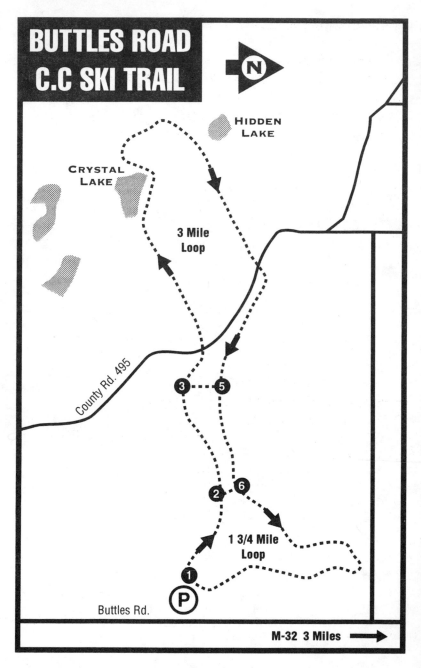

located about 6 miles due south of the area.

Information: Contact The Atlanta DNR Field Office, HCR 74, P.O. Box 30, Atlanta, MI 49709; ☎ (517) 785-4251.

Buttles Road Pathway

Distance: 6 miles
Trail: Single track
Direction: Clockwise

The trail rolls through Posts 2 and 3 in about a mile of easy riding. It starts out in a Jack pine forest with a few hardwoods mixed in. Quickly you come to the rim of a long, pine-studded, cylindrical-shaped sinkhole valley, which you continue to skirt all the way to Post 3, reached at *Mile 1*.

Leaving Post 3 the trail begins a 3-mile segment that rolls through a lot of open area and skirts a couple of lakes near the backside of the loop. Quickly you cross County Road-495 and continue to roll through the sparsely wooded countryside for about a mile. Shortly before you see Crystal Lake, the trail begins to climb a little more and enters some hardwoods on a ridge above the lake. Watch the plunge down the notch in the ridge, which you have to cross. It's rutted and sandy.

A quick drop to lake level and back up the other side takes care of the only real hill you encounter on this ride. It's an equally tough, sandy climb up the other side.

The pathway continues to climb several more little hills by Hidden Lake and then again crosses County Road-495 near *Mile 4* of the ride. Turn right after crossing the road. It's an easy half mile over to Post 5. If you missed Post 4, so did I.

Post 6 is reached near *Mile 5* and here the trail rims the other side of the valley you rode along on the way out. It's 1.5 miles back to the parking lot from Post 6. The trail dips down into a little sinkhole valley as it heads north. It skirts around another larger and deeper valley before heading south through a hardwood forest to the parking lot.

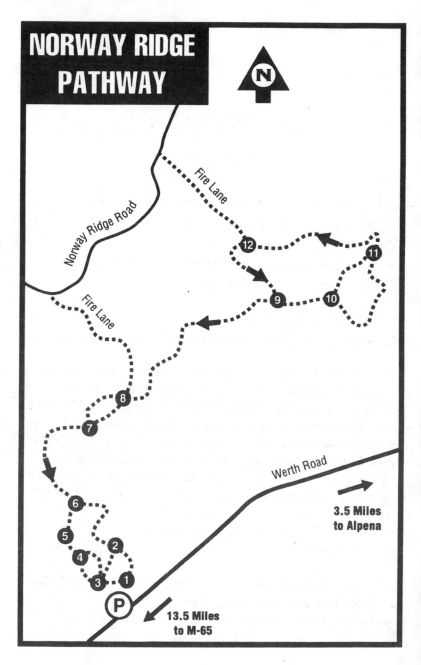

NORWAY RIDGE PATHWAY

Norway Ridge Road

Fire Lane

Fire Lane

12

11

9

10

8

7

6

5

2

4

3

1

P

Werth Road

3.5 Miles to Alpena

13.5 Miles to M-65

Norway Ridge Pathway

County: Alpena
Total Mileage: 7.4 miles
Terrain: Level to slightly rolling through pine and hardwood forest
Fees: None
Difficulty: Easy

For a weekend of riding in the Alpena area, combine the Norway Ridge Pathway with the nearby Chippewa Hills Pathway.

This trail system is an easier ride than Chippewa Hills but a scenic and pleasant outing as you alternate between majestic red pines and hardwood stands along low ridges. The trail is divided into three distinct loops with two-way spurs connecting them.

Be prepared for a few muddy spots. The ideal time to ride this trail is in late summer or fall, when conditions are normally dryer. As with other trails this far north, autumn colors make this a spectacular ride from early to mid-October.

Getting There: From US-23, on the south side of Alpena, head southwest on Werth Road. The trailhead will be passed in 4.5 miles.

39

Information: Contact the Atlanta DNR Field Office, Rte. 1, P.O. Box 30, Atlanta, MI 49709; ☎ (517) 785-04251.

Norway Ridge Pathway

Distance: 5.6 miles
Trail: Single and double track
Direction: Counter clockwise

The trail heads out of the small trailhead parking lot to the right as it rolls quickly through a stand of beautiful red pine to Post 2. Continue straight ahead for a third of a mile to Post 6.

The left fork at 6 takes you back to the parking lot or later serves as your return trail. Continue straight ahead as the two-way connecting spur rolls through a combination of open fields and woods, reaching Post 7 at **Mile 0.8**.

It's only a couple hundred yards over to Post 8. It's easier (and drier) in either direction to follow the left fork as the right fork plunges off a little ridge where at the bottom an innocent looking mud hole waits to suck you in. I rode this during a dry summer and it was still hub deep.

From Post 8 the trail winds through the woods for a half mile to Post 9, where this two-way portion ends. You head straight for Post 10, reached just past **Mile 2**. The trail rolls up and down a small pine covered ridge line and then again becomes a two-way track a third of a mile before the junction.

Head right and ride around the short loop, a ride of a little over a half mile. Shortly after leaving Post 11, you pass some benches and a firepit. Norway Ridge is a popular ski trail and this rest area is set up for Nordic skiers. Post 12 is reached at **Mile 2.4**, where a trail, that used to be part of the system, departs to the right.

A few years ago this system was rerouted and subsequently renumbered. The long section coming up between 10 and 9 is new but does uses a portion of this older section. Leaving Post 12, the trail takes you down into another wet section before returning to Post 11.

Return to Post 10 via the short section of two-way trail, and then head right for the new section of the trail. This 1.5-mile stretch of trail meanders along some pretty, open ridgelines. For most riders it is a welcomed change after the last 2 to 3 miles which has been through a canopy of hardwood and pine with very little daylight at times.

Just before **Mile 4**, the trail drops off the ridge to skirt a gate and cross a bridge. It's a short ride back to Post 9 once you crest the next ridge.

The mile to Post 6 retraces your earlier route. Post 6 is reached at **Mile 5.2** and from there you head right as the trail gently descends to the parking lot, passing through Posts 5, 3 and 2.

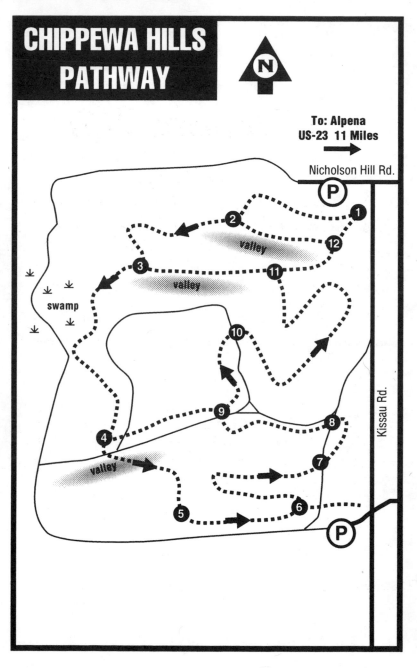

CHIPPEWA HILLS PATHWAY

To: Alpena
US-23 11 Miles

Nicholson Hill Rd.

valley

valley

swamp

valley

Kissau Rd.

Chippewa Hill Pathway

County: Alpena
Total Mileage: 8 miles
Terrain: Rolling hardwood hills and long, deep valleys
Fees: None
Difficulty: Moderate

Located on the eastern side of the state, Chippewa Hills Pathway is best known as a scenic destination for cross country skiers. But outside of winter, the trail also offers mountain bikers a firm, single track that rolls through the scenic hardwood hills dominating this area, making it a fun ride of mostly moderate climbs and descents. Best of all, usage of the system by bikers is relatively light.

The system totals 8 miles along four loops that includes trail maps and directional arrows at intersections, a scattering of benches and some scenic overlooks along the edges of the valleys that dominate the area. The trail does cross a number of two-track and forest roads but is easy to follow.

Combine this ride with nearby Norway Ridge or Black Mountain, then spend some time exploring the Huron shoreline and it makes a great weekend trip.

Getting There: Located southeast of Alpena, take Nicholson Hill Road west off US-23 for 12 miles. Turn south on Kissau Road and the parking lot is on the right. A second trailhead is located further south on Kissau Road.

Information: Contact the Atlanta DNR Field Office, P.O. Box 30, Atlanta, MI 49709; ☎ (517) 785-4252.

Chippewa Hills Pathway

Distance: 6.6 Miles
Trail: Single track
Direction: Counter clockwise

The outer perimeter of this scenic trail system is a 6.6-mile ride that appears more rugged than it actually is. There is little evidence of civilization in the area as the trail rolls up and down the forested hills, often skirting deep valleys.

You begin with a long downhill in the first half mile as the trail descends to Post 2. The trail drops a little more then starts to wind its way to Post 3, ending with a short, steep climb just before reaching the intersection at *Mile 1.2*.

Head right at Post 3. The trail first skirts a deep valley then quickly descends to cross the western end of it. After passing a swamp, you ride through a series of five or six roller coaster hills, encountering some good climbs and fast downhills.

The trail levels out momentarily at Post 4 then begins a long, gentle downhill run. You skirt another swamp, cross a bridge and begin a long two-tiered uphill climb to Post 5, which is reached at *Mile 2.7*. You may have to go around a gate after crossing the bridge, which is sometimes locked.

The next mile to Post 8 is gentle riding. The trail climbs steadily but not steeply to Post 6, where you head left. The other spur connects with a little-used trailhead and parking lot. If you were having problems, with either your bike or legs, head out on this spur and take a left on Kissau Road. It's the shortest way back to the trailhead parking lot.

Post 7 is reached following a long downhill run and a short uphill climb across a rough two-track. The trail continues to roll as you climb through a beautiful stand of aspen followed by a long downhill run through a thick stand of pine to Post 8, reached at **Mile 3.7**. Just before reaching the signpost you cross the two-track again.

It's nearly 3 miles to the trailhead from Post 8. The trail steadily climbs until Post 11, regaining the elevation lost in the first three sections, but does so gently. Because of the constant roll, it hardly seems like you're climbing and makes for a pleasant ride. Along the way you cross a couple of two-tracks. The final half mile from Post 11 is flat and easy as you skirt another deep valley just before arriving at Post 12 and then the trailhead.

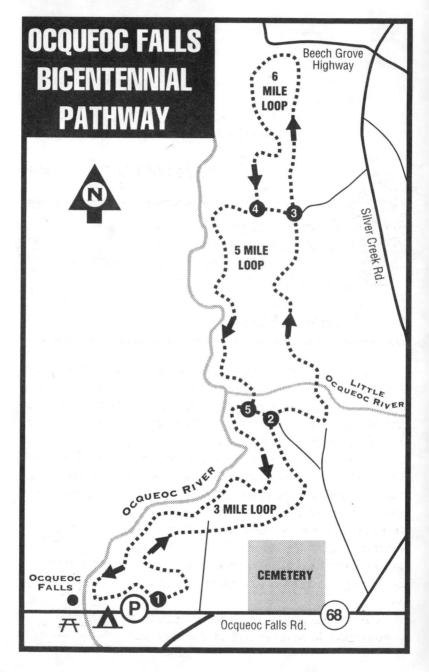

OCQUEOC FALLS BICENTENNIAL PATHWAY

N

Beech Grove Highway

6 MILE LOOP

4   3

5 MILE LOOP

Silver Creek Rd.

LITTLE OCQUEOC RIVER

5   2

OCQUEOC RIVER

3 MILE LOOP

CEMETERY

OCQUEOC FALLS

1

68

Ocqueoc Falls Rd.

Ocqueoc Falls Pathway

County: Presque Isle
Total Mileage: 6 miles
Terrain: Gently rolling trail, waterfalls and the Ocqueoc River
Fees: None
Difficulty: Easy

Ocqueoc Falls is one of only two waterfalls in the Lower Peninsula and certainly the most scenic. The pretty cascade is located just below the parking lot and is part of a dayuse area. Unless you sneak a peak in before the ride, you won't actually see the falls until the end of the ride.

More than just the falls, this is a very scenic area dominated by the river valley with its towering pines and hardwoods. You ride out along a ridge above the valley for some incredible views, and then return along the river. The riding is very easy. The 6-mile trail system includes two crossover spurs for loops of 3 miles, 5 miles and 6 miles. The 3-mile loop is the most scenic by far, hugging the river along most the second half.

The dayuse area around the falls can be a popular place in summer and fall. But once you hit the trails, most likely you will encounter few if any people, especially on the back loops. Most hikers seldom venture beyond the first loop.

This pathway and the Black Mountain area are two of my favorite fall rides. Staying at an area lodge or in one of the three nearby campgrounds makes for a nice weekend of riding. On the south side of Ocqueoc Falls Road is the Ocqueoc Falls Campground, an extremely scenic 14-site rustic facility. Many of the sites are on the edge of a high bank overlooking the river.

Getting There: The trailhead is located just west of the M-68 and Ocqueoc Falls Road junction, about 11 miles due west of Rogers City and US-23.

Information: Contact the DNR Gaylord Regional Office, P.O. Box 667, Gaylord, MI 49735; ☎ (517) 732-3541.

Ocqueoc Falls Pathway
Distance: 6 miles
Trail: Single track and some double track
Direction: Counter clockwise
Head north from the posted trailhead in the parking lot. Quickly the firm, single-track trail arrives at a T-intersection. Head right over to Post 2. For the next 1.5 miles the trail winds along a ridge offering overlook after overlook of the scenic river valley flanked by high hills on both sides.

At Post 2 at **Mile 1.5**, a left takes you down a gentle slope to Post 5 and the return along the river for a 3-mile ride. To the right, the trail continues to roll along the ridge towards Post 3 at **Mile 2.5**, where it quickly descends to cross the Little Ocqueoc River.

For the next 3 miles the trail meanders back and forth between small wooded pockets, meadows and small undulating hills. Along this section the trail reverts to some old two-tracks, which crisscross the area. At times it is difficult to figure out which way

Ocqueoc Falls, one of only two cascades in the Lower Peninsula.

to go. However, it would be tough to get lost as the area is bordered by Silver Creek Road to the east and the Ocqueoc River to the west.

At Post 3, you can again return to the trailhead for a 5 mile ride or head right to complete the final loop. The trail heads out for a half-mile than loops back to Post 4 through more of the same type terrain.

At Post 4, at **Mile 3.5**, the trail swings right. The pathway continues along a small ridge above the river for a half-mile before descending to the trout stream. Just before the descent you are rewarded with the first real, unobstructed glimpse of this scenic little river at **Mile 4**. It's a beautiful spot.

For the next 2 miles the trail stays mostly along side the river as it rolls through post 5 and continues south towards the falls. When you reach the falls, this is another scenic spot that deserves some viewing time. While not big by Upper Peninsula standards, Ocqueoc Falls makes for the perfect place to end a ride, especially on a hot summer afternoon.

The parking lot is just up the hill. This will be the longest climb you have on the ride.

Black Mountain Recreation Area

County: Cheboygan and Presque Isle
Total Mileage: 31 miles of trails plus numerous forest roads
Terrain: Heavily wooded ridges and hills
Fees: Donations
Difficulty: Moderate to strenuous

If you're looking for a great weekend mountain bike retreat, look no further than the Black Mountain Forest Recreation Area. Located 15 miles southeast of Cheboygan or 20 miles northeast of Rogers City, this remote tract offers miles of single-track, double track and dirt roads for riding.

Black Mountain looms over the east side of massive Black Lake. It's a series of long, wooded ridges that peak to a high point of 925 feet and parallel the Lake Huron shoreline six miles away. You catch glimpses of the Great Lake's shining waters from some vantage points along the trail. The ridge was deposited here about 10,000 years ago as the last ice age drew to a close. Today, most of this striking landscape forms the 9,000-acre Black Mountain Forest Recreation Area.

Constructed in 1993, this 31-mile trail system was designed for cross country skiers but is open to mountain bikers, hikers and horseback riding. The number of loops and possible rides is almost endless but keep in mind there are also 60 miles of ORV trails as well as a scramble area for motorcycles and ATVs. These motorized trail users aren't allowed on your trail system, and you really want to stay off theirs. You also can't ride the area during the winter months of December through March.

Beautiful Black Lake Campground, a rustic state forest facility with sites overlooking the water, is just off Doriva Beach Road and near the western trailhead for the trail system. Onaway State Park is on the southern end of Black Lake and features a modern campground, a nice beach and picnic area.

Within a short distance of the northern trailhead on Twin Lakes Road is Twin Lakes Campground, another rustic facility, while nearby is Chateau Lodge (☎ 616-625-9322). Located at the base of the mountain on Twin Lakes Road, the lodge offers a comfortable atmosphere that fits well with the area. The restaurant is quite nice and serves excellent fare. Its wall of windows looks out over Twin Lakes and Black Mountain and is very picturesque in the evening as the sun sets.

Getting There: From I-75 take exit 310 at Indian River and head east on M-68 to Onaway reached in 29 miles. In Onaway, north on M-211 to County Road-489 and then follow the "Black Mountain Trail" signs. There are four trailheads to the pathway. The southern trailhead is on County Road-489, nine miles from Onaway, and the western one is on Doriva Beach Road, which splits off from the county road. The northern trailhead on Twin Lakes Road, west of its junction with Doriva Beach Road. The tract is almost split in half by Black Mountain Road. The fourth trailhead is located here.

Information: Contact the Atlanta DNR Field Office, P.O. Box 30, Atlanta, MI 49709-9605; ☎ (517) 785-4252.

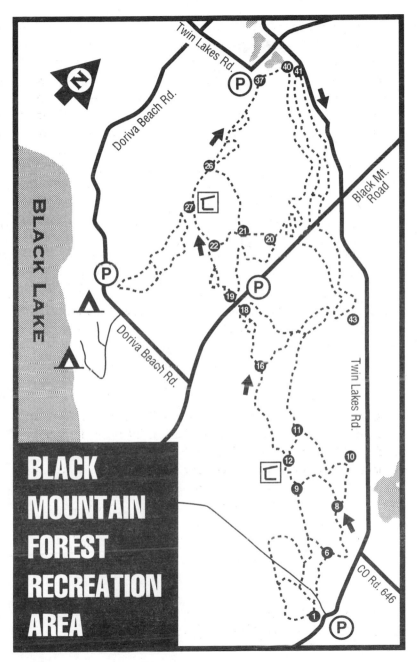

Top Of The Mountain Ride

Distance: 12.2 miles
Trail: Double track and forest roads
Direction: Clockwise

This route first heads southeast along Twin Lakes Road, a dirt road, and then returns over the top of the Black Mountain. Twin Lakes Road parallels the base of the ridge and offers riding that is easy and scenic through thick forests. You can park at the northern trailhead on Twin Lakes for this ride or the Chateau Lodge if you're staying there.

Head south on Twin Lakes Road for six miles to the southern trailhead, which is less than a mile beyond the County Road-646 intersection. At the trailhead there is a vault toilet, large trail map and a donation pipe. Please drop some money into the pipe for trail maintenance.

Follow the pathway from Post 1 to Post 2 and up to Post 6. It's a long, sandy two-track that climbs steadily uphill for about a half mile. Once up on top the trail condition tends to improve and the surface is much harder. The trail will continue to improve with age and use.

As you round the corner to Post 8, there are a couple of places you can catch a glint of Lake Huron's Hammond Bay in the distance. Benches located here make this a good spot to stop and rest after that exhausting climb.

It's a long, gentle half mile downhill over to Post 8, reached at **Mile 7.3** into the ride. The trail to the right here leads to Post 10 and is a longer, more hilly route to Post 18, which is the trailhead on Black Mountain Road.

I like riding over to Post 9 and continuing through Post 12 and Post 16 to Post 18. After a quick uphill from Post 8, the trail becomes flat to gently rolling. At Post 12, you'll find a beautiful three-sided shelter, one of two built by the DNR in the recreation area. Grills and a firepit are located near the shelter, making this a great spot for a picnic lunch.

After a rest stop at the shelter, continue on over to Post 16 and Post 18, reached at **Mile 9.7**. It's 1.5 miles of easy riding as you meander across the top through thick forests yielding no views.

As you cross Black Mountain Road, a dirt road, the easier trail runs though Posts 24, 23 and over to 22. If you want some good hills try heading from Post 19 over to Post 20 and back to Post 22. It's about a mile longer, and offers some challenging hills.

The half-mile, mostly downhill run from Post 22 to Post 27 follows an old two-track and is a great ride. Post 27, reached at **Mile 10.7**, is where you'll find the other three-sided shelter and is the junction to the trail from Doriva Beach Road, near the Black Lake Campground.

From the shelter it's 1.5 miles back to Twin Lake and the Chateau. The trail is mostly flat to rolling for fairly easy riding. Overall you will have ridden about 12 to 15 miles depending on the trails you choose riding over Black Mountain.

Black Mountain Challenge

Distance: 6.2 miles
Trail: Double track

For a strenuous-rated ride try the advanced trail sections between Posts 40 and 43 that in the winter is a skate-ski loop. This 6.2-mile loop winds through hilly terrain that is a challenge to negotiate as the trail rolls up and down the heavily forested flanks of the ridges. If the roller coaster ride becomes tiring, you can always find a two-track that quickly leads you back down to Twin Lakes Road and an easy return.

Central Highlands Region

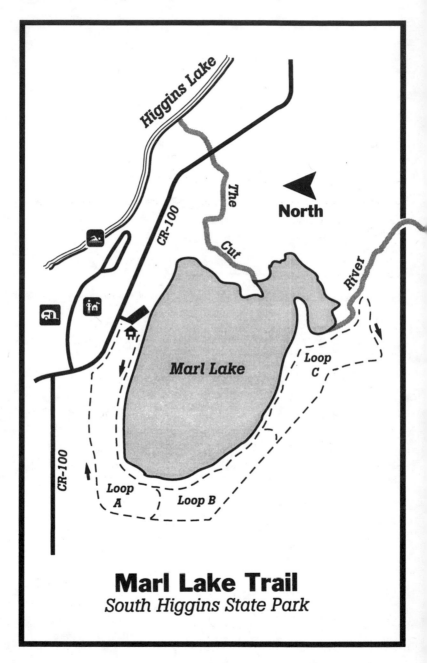

Marl Lake Trail
South Higgins State Park

Marl Lake Trail

County: Roscommon
Total Mileage: 5.5 Miles
Terrain: Flat, forested bottom land along Marl Lake
Fees: Daily vehicle entry fee or annual state park pass
Difficulty: Easy

South Higgins Lake State Park is one of the busiest and most popular parks in the Lower Peninsulas but a quick escape lies right across the road from the park's main entrance. The Marl Lake Trail is a delightful and easy ride along the shores of its namesake lake yet usually avoids the crush of humanity found at the park's campground and beach throughout much of the summer.

The state park's popularity is due to the large, modern campground and beach on the south shore of Higgins Lake. This 9,600-acre lake is one of the first bodies of water that you come to after entering the northern highlands, which start about West Branch. Houghton Lake, larger at 20,044 acres, is located just a few miles south. Both offer a typical "up north" lake setting...crystal clear waters surrounded by rolling forested hills.

Marl Lake is much smaller, but equally scenic. It's surrounded by lowlands with a mixed cover of conifer and hardwood trees. The Cut River flows out of the northwest end of the lake on its way to Houghton Lake. Lake views are abundant through the first couple of miles of the pathway.

Because of the campground, Marl Lake is a popular pathway on weekends with hikers. Midweek is a better time to ride. If you ride on the weekend be prepared to go slow and work your way around the walkers, many of them families.

This trail should be ridden only during the dry season, summer and early fall, because of the lowlands and the exposed root systems along sections of the pathway.

Getting There: From I-75, depart at exit 239 and head west on M-18, but immediately turn north (right) onto Robinson Lake Road. Robinson will curve west into County Road 100. The trailhead parking lot is located on CR-100 just across the road from South Higgins Lake State Park.

Information: Contact South Higgins State Park, 106 State Park Drive, Roscommon, MI 48853; ☎ (517) 821-6374.

Marl Lake Trail
Distance: 5.5 miles
Trail: Single and double track
Direction: Clockwise

The pathway is color coded. Follow the blue marker symbols for the long ride.

The view from the parking area of Marl Lake is one of the best for enjoying the entire lake. You're located about in the middle of the lake's north shore, which is close to a half mile across and about 2 miles in length. It's a popular fishing lake.

As you head south from the parking lot the pathway hugs the shoreline for a couple of miles. The first half mile is one of the most scenic sections. Lake views abound, and the pathway is flat and easy at this point as it winds through the trees along the lake shore. In a short distance you come to some bridging between the lake on the left and a beautiful lily-covered pond on the right.

Just before **Mile 1**, the green trail, a 2-mile loop, exits to the right. Stay left and get ready for some rough riding. The next 1.3 miles is a pretty technical section, involving riding around or over large tree roots covering the pathway. You have to bounce, bob and weave your way through this fun section. Knowing how to bunny-hop your bike over the larger roots would be helpful.

By the time you reach the Cut River you'll be ready for a break. It's intense riding because you have to constantly concentrate plotting your path through the maze of roots. At times you may feel like Libor Karas, the legendary Czechoslovakian Observed Trail World Champion.

At **Mile 1.6**, you pass the intersection where the red trail, a 3.5-mile loop, exits to the right. The roots finally head underground when you reach the Cut River at **Mile 2.3** miles. There's a bench available on the river bank, making this a pretty spot to relax after the "root" section.

The rest of the ride is a breeze. The pathway is flat and firm with just a few widely scattered roots crossing the wide trail. The cedars along the lake shore have given way to hardwoods. Basically the return pathway parallels the lakeshore on the way back, but far enough inland so you don't see either the lake or the outbound pathway on the way back.

You pass where the red trail again merges with the blue trail at **Mile 3.2**, and the green trail rejoins shortly after you pass **Mile 4**. Just before the green trail intersection, the pathway turns right, but a spur continues straight ahead to quickly connect with a dirt road. This intersection is not well marked. The first time I rode this, I ended up at the dirt road and had to back track.

After the green trail merges with the other two, it's about 1.3 miles back to the parking lot. This is a pretty section where the pathway rolls through some open meadows and across a small hill. The trail parallels CR-100 at the end. Just after **Mile 5**, a spur to the left leads over to the campground if you're staying there.

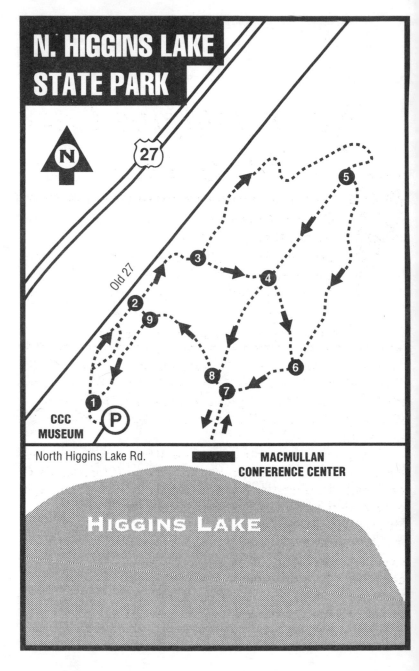

N. HIGGINS LAKE STATE PARK

N

27

Old 27

CCC
MUSEUM

P

North Higgins Lake Rd.

**MACMULLAN
CONFERENCE CENTER**

HIGGINS LAKE

North Higgins Lake State Park

County: Crawford
Total Mileage: 6.5 Miles
Terrain: Rolling pine covered hills with some hardwoods
Fees: Daily vehicle entry permit or annual state park pass
Difficulty: Easy to slightly moderate

There are three rides in the Roscommon area; Beaver Creek Trail in North Higgins Lake State Park, Tisdale Triangle and the Mari Lake Trail at South Higgins Lake State Park. They are all easy riding but Beaver Creek Trail is by far the best of the three, and the most interesting.

This 6.5-mile trail is a scenic ride with firm, long winding segments that flow through deep pine and hardwood forests. There's even informative interpretive signs strategically placed throughout the route that makes this ride a historically interesting one as well as scenic.

Also located within the state park are the Civilian Conservation Corps (CCC) Museum, detailing the important contributions this group has made to Michigan's natural resources, and the MacMullan Conference Center situated across North Higgins Lake Road. Both are open on a daily basis throughout the summer and fall. A 218-site, modern campground is situated along the lakeshore while vault toilets are located at the trailhead.

Getting There: North Higgins Lake State Park is on County Road-203, west of Roscommon between US-27 and I-75. From I-75, depart at exit 244 and head west. The trailhead is in the parking lot for the CCC Museum on the north side of the road.

Information: Contact North Higgins State Park, 11511 N. Higgins Lake Drive, Roscommon, MI 48653; ☎ (517) 821-6125.

Beaver Creek Trail
Distance: 6.5 miles
Trail: Single track
Direction: Clockwise

The wide trail begins along a row of pines that separate the parking lot and the CCC Museum. After swinging left through a pine stand the trail begins to gently climb to Post 2 in slightly less than a mile. The trail drops gradually for the next half mile to reach Post 3 at *Mile 1.5*. This is a fun section with some sweeping turns built in.

At the junction, Beaver Creek Trail heads north (left) to wind through an old pine forest for the next 3 miles. The pine needles provide a nice firm cushion as the trail weaves in and out of the trees. Along the back section you'll find a couple of "ancient" pines marked with plaques.

The first one you come to is a 132-year-old red pine, measuring nearly 80-inches in diameter. Further along the back part of this section is a white pine whose plaque states: "I first awoke to the distant sounds of a Civil War in 1863." It measures 108-inches in diameter. The top of the tree was lost in a man-made fire in 1908, but it still survives. Now that these two ancient ones are in a protected environment, depending on the whims of nature, they may survive another 300 years or so.

The Cone Barn at the CCC Museum in North Higgins Lake State Park, where the Beaver Creek Trail begins.

Shortly after the white pine you come to Post 5. The left fork, Beaver Creek Trail, is the easier and slightly shorter route to Post 6. The right fork that departs straight ahead is a short cut trail to Post 4 and involves a little more climbing.

Continuing on Beaver Creek Trail, it's a 1.4-mile ride to Post 6 along a trail that winds through a beautiful stand of pines. Once past the pines you start to climb and enter a stately oak forest near Post 6, reached at **Mile 4.2**. The trail then drops to Post 7 with a nice half-mile downhill stretch. Roll through Post 8 and proceed to make the longest climb of the ride as you work your way up to Post 9. The left at Post 7 takes you over to the MacMullan Conference Center.

The trail starts to drop again as you leave Post 9. It's a fast half-mile descent as you roll back into the field where you started. The parking lot is straight ahead.

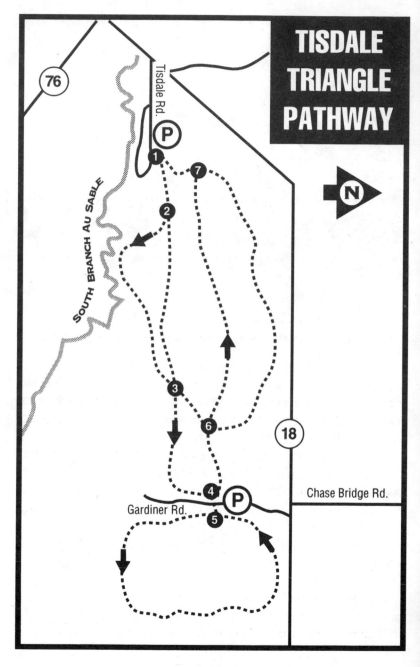

TISDALE TRIANGLE PATHWAY

Tisdale Triangle Pathway

County: Roscommon
Total Mileage: 8.4 miles
Terrain: Flat, mostly forested trails with some open areas on the back loop.
Fees: None
Difficulty: Easy

Tisdale Triangle Pathway is an easy system with little elevation change. The trail winds through mostly Jack pine for a pleasant ride, but one I wouldn't go out of my way for. But if you tack it on with the Beaver Creek Trail at North Higgins Lake for a full day of riding then it's worth the effort.

The entire system has 8.4 miles of trail along four loops. But keep in mind that Tisdale Triangle Pathway was designed and is maintained primarily for cross country skiers. The DNR office in Roscommon pays little attention to this pathway in the summer so it's possible the back portion of this pathway might be unsuitable for riding.

Getting There: The trailhead is located just north of Roscommon. From M-18, head east on Tisdale Road to the trailhead at the end of

Tisdale Triangle Pathway is an easy trail system with little elevation change. But for bikers heading north on I-75, it can be a quick ride to stretch the legs or get a little trail time in before nightfall.

the road.

Information: Contact the DNR Region II Headquarters, P.O. Box 218, Roscommon, MI 48653; ☎ (517) 275-5151.

Tisdale Triangle Pathway

Distance: 5.8 miles
Trail: double track
Direction: Counter clockwise

From the trailhead it's an easy third of a mile to Post 2. Take the right fork and follow the trail as it gently drops towards the South Branch of the Au Sable River. You never actually see the river because the trail stays in a pine and hardwood forest which becomes mostly hardwoods as you ride to past Post 3. The trail then climbs slightly to Post 4, reached at *Mile 1.6*.

Cross Gardner Road and proceed right at Post 5, directly across the gravel road. The trail remains totally flat as it makes a 2-mile circle. It crosses a few two-tracks and meanders in and out of clear-cut areas. About three-quarters of the way around the trail swings close to M-18, then ducks south, back to Post 5.

Again, cross Gardner road to Post 4, but this time proceed straight (right fork) to Post 6, reached at *Mile 4*. Here the trail heads in three directions. The forks straight ahead and to the right are very similar trails, with the right fork being slightly longer. The shorter trail seems to be the most popular choice with bikers but both take you to Post 7. From there it's only a couple hundred yards to the parking lot.

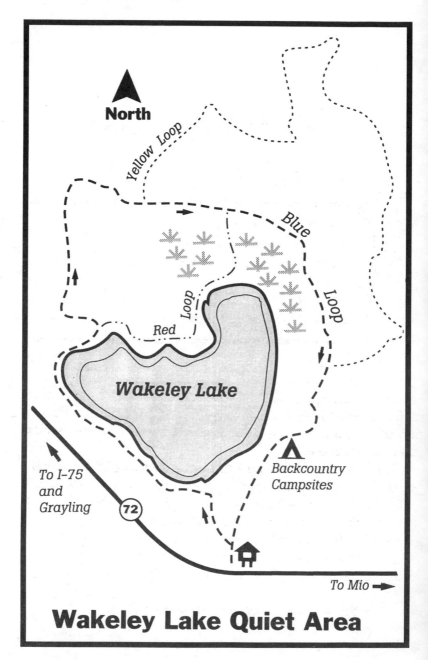

North

Yellow Loop

Blue

Loop

Red Loop

Wakeley Lake

Backcountry
Campsites

To I–75
and
Grayling

72

To Mio ➡

Wakeley Lake Quiet Area

Wakeley Lake Quiet Area

County: Crawford
Total Mileage: 16.5 miles
Terrain: Rolling, forested hills and Wakeley Lake
Fees: None
Difficulty: Easy to moderate

The U.S. Forest Service has designated Wakeley Lake as a "quiet area." Portions of this 2,000-acre tract have also been set aside as a nesting area for loons and bald eagles. That's just two of 115 species of birds that can be spotted in the area. Blue Heron are often plentiful around the lake, streams and beaver ponds that dot the preserve.

This is a scenic area with Wakeley Lake serving as the center piece. The trail system is mostly easy riding with just a few small hills. There are three loops, all color coded. The Red Loop is 4 miles, the Blue Loop 5 miles and the Yellow Loop 7 miles. The basic difference in the routes is the length with the Blue and Red Loops being the most frequently marked and thus the easiest to follow.

The Yellow Loop is not marked nearly as well and is more difficult to follow, partly because the area is crisscrossed with abandoned two-tracks.

This extensive system of two-track roads, there is close to 30 miles, is being left in a natural state and is slowly overgrowing with brush. Most of the two-tracks can still be followed and offer adventurous riding. Carry a compass, however, because it's hard to figure out where you are once you get away from the lake. Much of it meanders through thick undergrowth and wet lands where there is lots of evidence of beaver and deer in the area.

This can also be a great family area. The terrain isn't demanding and members of the family, who don't want to ride, can always relax along the lake. Wakeley Lake is a trophy bass and bluegill fishery but keep in mind that the fishing is catch-and-release only with a ban on the use of live bait. The angling season and other regulations are posted at the parking lot.

Getting There: The trailhead parking lot is located on the north side of M-72, 15 miles east of Grayling and I-75.

Information: Contact the Mio Ranger District, Huron-Manistee National Forest, 401 Court St., Mio, MI 48647; ☎ (517) 826-3252.

Blue Loop

Distance: 5 miles
Trail: Single track and double track
Direction: Clockwise

From the parking area, head down the two-track for a 100 yards and then head west (left) on a single track trail. A gradual downhill run takes you to the edge of Wakeley Lake. It passes between the lake and a lily-covered pond on the left before climbing a series of small hills while rounding the southwest corner of the lake.

Just before **Mile 1** the trail swings north and briefly splits. The right fork plunges down into a steep, little valley and quickly up the other side. The left fork, slightly longer, meanders around

Wakeley Lake is a noted trophy fishery for bluegills and bass, the result of special catch-and-release regulations the U.S. Forest Service has imposed on it.

the ridge avoiding any hills.

At **Mile 1.2** an unmarked trail takes off to the left. It's a short-cut that will shave a quarter mile off your ride while avoiding the long, sandy uphill climb to the junction with the 4-mile Red Loop. If you don't plan on taking the shorter trail, you can avoid the climb with this spur.

The Blue Loop continues to roll over a series of small hills for a mile before reaching the junction where the Yellow Loop starts its odyssey through the hinterland. Ignore the intersecting trail from the left just beyond **Mile 2** as it dead ends at a road within a half-mile.

The Yellow Loop junction is reached at **Mile 2.4** and within a short distance, the Blue Loop crosses Wakeley Creek and then winds along a grassy marsh. The island-like areas tucked in between the lake and the marsh is where the loons nest. The red trail rejoins the blue trail at this point.

From here it's roughly 2 miles back to the parking lot. The final leg begins by climbing a low rise for a view of the lake from between the pines and then descends to skirt a swamp. You quickly re-enter the pines and pass the second junction with the Yellow Loop before breaking out at a lightly wooded hill overlooking the lake. The U.S. Forest Service maintains a handful of campsites in this lovely spot that include a vault toilet but no source of water. Nearby is where canoers and belly boat anglers enter the catch-and-release-only lake.

From the launch area a wide two-track heads south 0.3 mile back to the parking lot off M-72.

Red Loop

Distance: 4 miles
Trail: Single track and two-track
Direction: Clockwise

Begin by following the Blue Loop. The split between the two loops is reached at **Mile 1.4** where you follow the right fork to continue on the shorter Red Loop.

This trail climbs a low wooded rise along the lake for a good view of the water and then swings north and descends into an open marshy area; the designated nesting area for the loon population. Keep in mind this stretch is closed to the public from March 1 to July 1 to prevent bikers and hikers from disturbing the birds.

You cross the marshy area along a sandy dike before arriving at the return junction with the Blue Loop, 2 miles from the trailhead and parking lot on M-72.

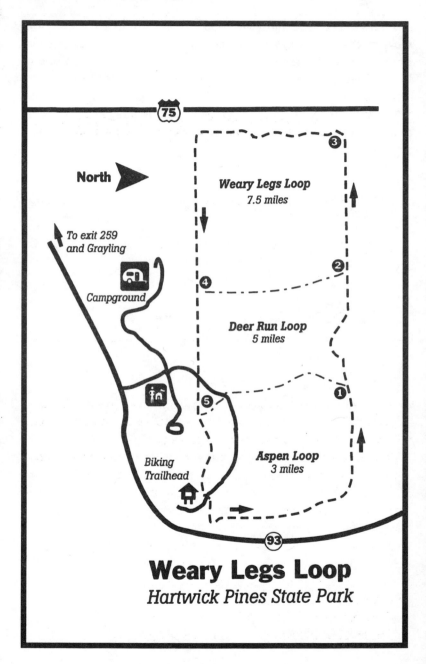

Weary Legs Loop
Hartwick Pines State Park

Hartwick Pines State Park

County: Crawford
Total Mileage: 10 miles
Terrain: Rolling forested hills
Fees: A daily vehicle entry permit or an annual State Park day pass.
Difficulty: Easy to moderate

Hartwick Pines, the Lower Peninsula's largest state park, has improved with age. An attractive new visitor center filled with interesting exhibits, displays and programs on Michigan's forests, a new modern campground and a new entrance and access road have combined to upgrade this old state park.

What hasn't changed, what probably needs no improvement, is the park's 10-mile system of mountain biking trails that winds through a portion of Hartwick Pines' beautiful 9,672 acres of rolling hills, overlooking the Au Sable River valley. Donated to the State of Michigan in 1927 by the Hartwick family, the tract contains a 49-acre forest of virgin white pine, that somehow was spared of the saws and axes of Michigan's logging era from 1840 to 1910.

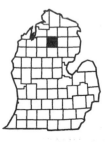

The mountain bike trails are located north of that tract and although the area was logged at the turn-of-the-century, the pines are still impressive and the woods they form is still a pleasant place to ride. The system is basically an 8-mile loop with two crossover spurs to form three different rides; the 3-mile Aspen Trail, the 5-mile Deer Run Trail and the 8-mile Weary Legs Trail.

The trails are also designated by color on the sign posts with red (Aspen) for easy, yellow (Deer Run) for intermediate and blue (Weary Legs) for advanced riders. Truth is, none of them are very hard and the few hills you encounter are moderate with straight downhill runs.

It's important to remember that the other trails in the park; AuSable Trail, Mertz Grade Trail and the Virgin Pines Trail that winds through the logging camp interpretive area, are off limits to mountain bikers. Nor can you ride your bike on other two-tracks within the park. You must stay on the designated bike trail system.

Getting There: The park is 7.5 miles northeast of Grayling. From I-75, depart at exit 259 and head north on M-93 to the park entrance. Bike trailhead is at the end of the park road in the Pines Picnic Area.

Information: Contact Hartwick Pines State Park, P.O. Box 3840, Grayling, MI 49738; ☎ (517) 348-7068.

Weary Legs Trail

Distance: 8 miles
Trail: Single track
Direction: Counter clockwise.

The trailhead is in the Pines Picnic Area on the north side of the entrance road and from there the trail departs north. The first intersection is reached at *Mile 2* after an easy ride that ends with a fast downhill to Post 1. The connecting trails; head south (left) to complete the short Aspen Trail and west to continue on the longer Weary Legs.

Another fast, sandy downhill leads you into a valley where Post 2, the site of an old logging camp, is located. A railroad spur used to run the length of this valley and huge white pine stumps still dominate the area...evidence of the great forest that once stood here. Post 2 is the junction for those completing the Deer Run Trail and is reached at *Mile 2.8*.

Continuing the long ride, you climb out of the valley on a long uphill as the trail heads over to Post 3. Once you crest the hill, the trail becomes a beautiful section that rolls through a "tunnel of trees." At Post 3, reached at *Mile 3.8*, the pathway swings south and parallels I-75 for about a mile. The interstate isn't visible, but highway sounds will undoubtedly remind you that it isn't far away.

At *Mile 5*, the trail swings east, away from the highway and into heavy forests. Here the trail suddenly gets wider along a section that can be muddy in the spring or after heavy rains.

You start a roller coaster section of hills at *Mile 5.5* that lead you to Post 4 in the valley, the junction with the connecting Deer Run Trail. Proceed across the valley and up into more small hills. The roller coaster ride continues as you cross the entrance road up into the low hills that surround the visitor center and logging camp replica. It's roughly a half mile from the spur that heads over to the visitor center to the Pines Picnic area.

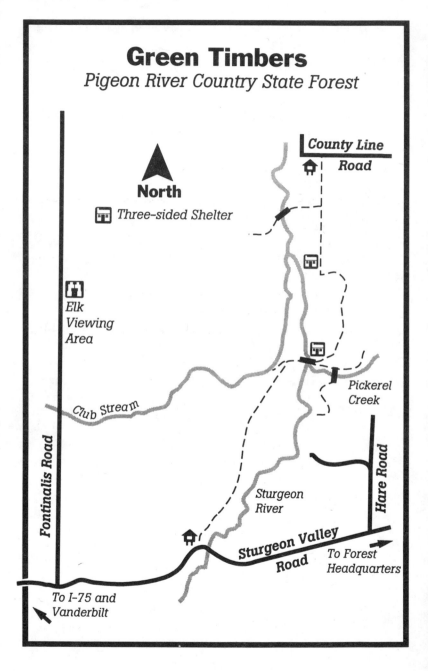

Green Timbers
Pigeon River Country State Forest

North

Three-sided Shelter

County Line Road

Elk Viewing Area

Club Stream

Pickerel Creek

Fontinalis Road

Hare Road

Sturgeon River

Sturgeon Valley Road

To Forest Headquarters

To I-75 and Vanderbilt

Green Timbers Recreation Area

County: Otsego
Total Mileage: 15 to 20 miles
Terrain: Rolling to hilly with wooded and open meadows
Fees: None
Difficulty: Easy to moderate

The Pigeon River Country State Forest offers a vast wooded area, almost 100,000 acres, for a variety of recreational uses, from trout fishing and camping to hiking and elk watching. Among the many users, of course, are mountain bikers.

There are a variety of trails to choose from. The 77-mile High Country Pathway winds through the heart of Pigeon River Country while the popular Shingle Mill Pathway is an 11-mile trail system on both sides of the Pigeon River.

What's not well known is that nearby Green Timbers Recreation Area offers some of the most scenic vistas and best habitat for wildlife viewing in the area...all accessible by bike.

The trails consist of old two-tracks, some well established, some barely visible. They are not marked. It's definitely a backcountry experience. Take along a map that can be obtained from forest headquarters, a compass and a sense

Green Timbers Cabin in Pigeon River Country State Forest.

of direction. If you can read land formations and translate them to a map, you shouldn't have a problem.

Green Timbers is a designated a "quiet area," which means no motorized vehicles within the boundaries. The wild, beautiful Sturgeon River flows through the middle of this 6,300-acre tract, which is home to elk, deer, bear and a variety of game birds.

The tract, originally developed as a hunting and fishing resort for McLouth Steel in the 1940s, was acquired by the state in 1982. The land was extensively logged, burned and grazed by cattle and sheep in the 1950s, which is still evident to the observant eye.

Today about 55 percent of Green Timbers is covered with a second growth of northern Michigan hardwoods, cedar and red and white pine. The remaining open grasslands, dotted with ancient pine stumps and single trees, offer wonderful opportunities for elk viewing.

This ride is along some of the best two-track in the recreation area. It begins at Sturgeon Valley Road and ends 4 miles later at Honeymoon Cabin, where it's possible to spend the night if you haul in the gear. Total ride on this point-to-point trail is 8 miles, including the return to your car.

Getting There: From I-75, depart at exit 290 and head south into Vanderbilt. Head east on Sturgeon Valley Road and the main trailhead for Green Timbers will be reached in 7 miles, just before you cross the Sturgeon River. The trailhead is merely a two-track with a locked gate across it and limited parking. The other trailhead is at an elk viewing area overlooking a huge meadow off Fontinalis Road.

Information: Continue another 7.5 miles east along Sturgeon Valley Road and follow the signs to reach the Pigeon River Country State Forest Headquarters (☎ 517-983-4101) on Twin Lakes Road. The office maintains irregular hours but there is a information display outside.

Honeymoon Cabin
Distance: 8 miles round trip
Trail: Double track
Direction: North from Sturgeon Valley Road
From the trailhead off of Sturgeon Valley Road, the two-track heads north along the river valley, although you don't actually see the river until you cross it. Most of this lower trail is through the woods. At **Mile 2**, you come to a "T" junction where you head right and shortly cross the river on a former vehicle bridge. On the other side is Green Timbers Cabin. This three-sided shelter is in a lovely spot, overlooking a lightly wooded bend in the river. The cabin is open to the public and features a fireplace and benches inside.

This is one of two such shelters within the tract, both are extremely popular with backpackers and winter campers looking for an overnight experience. The second one, Honeymoon Cabin, is located on a ridge overlooking the Sturgeon River Valley. It's 1.5

Elk in the meadows of the Green Timber Recreation Area of the Pigeon River Country State Forest. (Michigan DNR photo)

miles north of Green Timbers Cabin on the river. They are available on a first-come basis.

To reach the second shelter continue along the two-track as it curves behind the shelter and quickly climbs into wooded hills along the east side of the river.

The trail meanders through the woods and into an extensive

clear-cut area. At about **Mile 3.5** the trail forks. Take the left fork and proceed up the ridge in front of you to arrive at Honeymoon Cabin at **Mile 4**. This shelter is well named as the view from the ridgeline is stunning during autumn colors.

At this point most bikers simply back track to Sturgeon Valley Road and their car.

The alternative is to continue north along the ridge as the trail drops back down to the Sturgeon River, eventually crossing another bridge. Head west from here towards the elk viewing area off of Fontinalis Road.

It's a 3-mile ride up to that parking lot from the Sturgeon River. Most of this trail is through open grass lands and offers the opportunity to possibly spot wildlife. The trail is hard to follow at times. The old two-tracks, without constant use, are slowly disappearing. I found most of the two tracks to be negotiable, and most corresponded to the map. From the parking lot you can return to your car by heading south on Fontinalis Road and east on Sturgeon Valley Road for a complete loop of 13 miles.

Don't try and come back along the trails along the east side of the river from the river shelter. They aren't maintained and do not extend all the way to Sturgeon Valley Road, even though they appear to on the map. I ended up having to bushwhack through heavy brush carrying my bike.

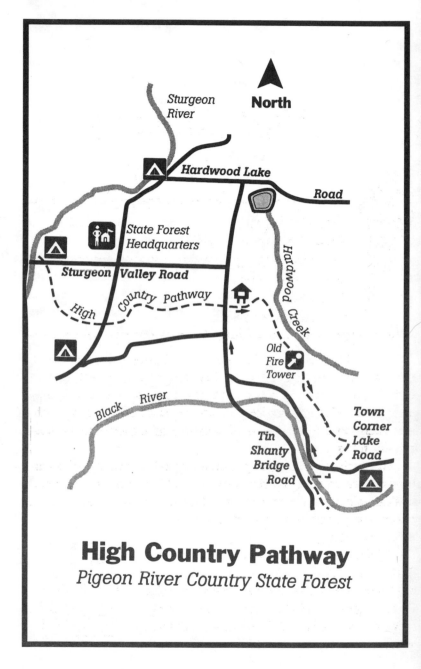

High Country Pathway
Pigeon River Country State Forest

High Country Pathway

County: Otsego
Total Mileage: 5.7 miles
Terrain: Rolling forested ridges overlooking Black River valley
Fees: None
Difficulty: Moderate

The High Country Pathway is a 77-mile loop that winds through the scenic Pigeon River Country and Mackinaw state forests. Although open to mountain bikes, it was built as a backpacking trail to offer hikers a long, multi-day trail. Few trails in southern Michigan offer this kind of backpacking experience as most are day hikes.

The pathway cuts through some rugged terrain as well as areas that are often wet and muddy. Overall I wouldn't recommend the pathway for mountain biking unless you know the terrain. But there are portions that lend themselves to mountain biking.

Following is a description of a circle ride that encompasses a portion of the High Country Pathway and a return along the scenic Black River. Segments of the pathway pass along a ridge with some beautiful overlooks of the river valley. You even pass an old fire tower that is

now open to the public. From the tower you can literally see for miles and enjoy an incredible view of Pigeon River Country.

Getting There: From I-75, depart at exit 290 and head south. In Vanderbilt, head east on Sturgeon Valley Road for 11 miles and then right on Tin Shanty Bridge Road. Continue south for 1.5 miles to where the pathway crosses Tin Shanty Road. There is a forest road that pulls into a clearing just off the road where you can park and begin the ride.

Information: Contact Pigeon River Country State Forest, 9966 Twin Lakes Rd., Vanderbilt, MI 49759; ☎ (517) 983-4101.

High Country Pathway
Tin Shanty Bridge Road to Town Corner
Distance: 5.7 miles
Trail: Single track and forest road
Direction: Counter clockwise

Heading south from the trailhead the first half mile is through heavy forest with lots of roots and small logs. It's usually dry and suitable for riding, but be careful just the same.

The next mile or so the pathway is more open as it rolls along the fern-covered forest floor. It climbs slowly and steadily but is not steep. Just before **Mile 2** you begin a steep climb that takes you up to the old fire tower. It's a great lunch spot. Take the time to climb the tower as the view is worth all the steps up.

At this point the uphill climbs on the route are done with the exception of a couple of quick ascents, before dropping down on the road. The trail meanders along the ridge for the next 1.5 miles before heading down.

In the next half mile, you come to a couple of other over-looks, which are okay but not nearly as good as what you see from the fire tower. The first one is marked and offers a very limited view. The second one is not marked, but occurs when the trail comes to an "T" intersection at **Mile 2.8**. The pathway

Mountain bikers on the High Country Pathway, just south of the firetower in Pigeon River Country State Forest.

heads left, but take the short spur to the right. It leads to a bench and beautiful overlook of the lush river valley and open highland meadows on the other side. It's a much better view than the marked one and is only a quarter mile down the trail mile.

It's a mile descent to the road after leaving the overlook. Make sure you go right at the Town Corner Campground fork. The left fork takes you over to the campground, which is a mile away. Travel as lightly as possible through this section, although it's a nice downhill run. I've come across elk herds here.

When you reach Town Corner Lake Road at **Mile 3.7**, turn right and follow it to a "T" intersection. Again, turn right, and follow Tin Shanty Bridge Road to where you started. It's about 2 miles once you reach the road back to where the High County Pathway crosses it.

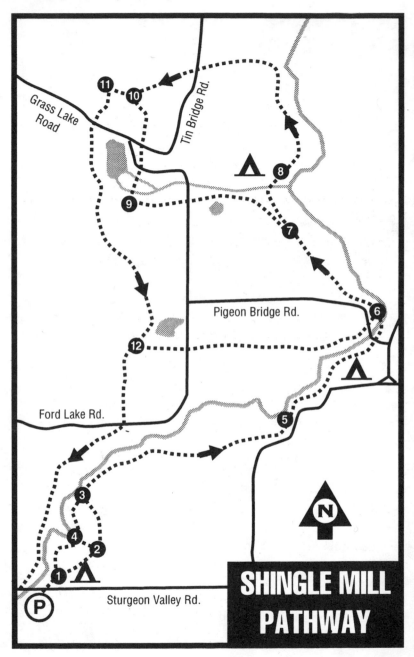

Grass Lake Road

Tin Bridge Rd.

Pigeon Bridge Rd.

Ford Lake Rd.

N

SHINGLE MILL
PATHWAY

Sturgeon Valley Rd.

P

Shingle Mill Pathway

County: Cheboygan and Otsego
Total Mileage: 18 miles
Terrain: Low swamp-like areas, ridges, scenic vistas and the Pigeon River valley
Fees: None
Difficulty: Moderate to strenuous

Home to a variety of animal life indigenous to the region, the Pigeon River Country State Forest boasts the largest elk herd east of the Mississippi. Several times, while riding in the area, I've seen these magnificent animals, which is quite a sight for those of us used to encountering "small" deer on the trail.

The 98,000-acre state forest is a rugged land of contrasts in both topography and weather. Both the highest and lowest temperatures ever recorded in Michigan occurred in this region, ranging from a bone chilling minus 51 degrees to a sultry high of 112 degrees. The average mean temperature is a chilly 42 degrees. Few areas better epitomize the term "up north" than the vast Pigeon River Country.

You may be surprised to see the rivers in this region flowing north. During the later stages of the glacial retreat they flowed south with torrential force creating the present deep river valleys. As the last of the glaciers retreated into the Great Lakes basin, they uncovered channels to the north, causing a directional change in the flow.

Designed as a pathway within the High Country Pathway, Shingle Mills features five loops from 2 to 11 miles with all of them being nice single track. Some of the trail meanders along the banks of the wild, beautiful Pigeon River.

Getting There: From I-75, depart at exit 290 and head south. In Vanderbilt, head east on Sturgeon Valley Road to reach the trailhead in 9 miles at the Pigeon River Bridge. The parking lot is located on the south side of the road. The trail actually begins at the back of the state forest campground across the road from the parking area.

Information: Contact Pigeon River Country State Forest, 9966 Twin Lakes Rd., Vanderbilt, MI 49759; ☎ (517) 983-4101.

Shingle Mill Pathway

Distance: 11 miles
Trail: Single track
Direction: Counter clockwise

Heading north out of the campground, the trail rolls quickly through Posts 1, 2 and 3. Shortly after heading right at Post 3, you wind along the scenic Pigeon River for a short distance. Head back up along a wooded ridge for the next mile or so before crossing through the DNR Forest Headquarters at **Mile 2.2**. This impressive log lodge is a great place to stop for conversation and information on the area.

The pathway rolls up and down a series of small hills before reaching Pigeon River Campground at **Mile 3**. Continue through the campground and head left over the river on the bridge at the north end. This is also a pretty spot for a break. Immediately after crossing the bridge, the trail swings right along the river. Post 6 is just ahead.

After a quick climb, the trail continues snaking along a high ridge above the river, reaching Post 7 at **Mile 4.5**. The 11-mile ride plunges down the steep bank. The 10-mile loop continues straight ahead past a sinkhole lake, over to Post 9, around Grass Lake and climbs to post 10 where the two trails merge once more.

For those continuing on the 11-mile ride, be careful of the descent. It's steep, narrow and sandy. Cross over a tributary that feeds the Pigeon River to arrive at Cornwall Flats and Post 8. The flats was the site of an abandoned, turn-of-the-century lumber mill that was in operation only for a few years. It's a beautiful spot that overlooks a tag alder swamp, once a large mill pond. As you leave this peaceful spot, the trail begins a series of long, arduous climbs through the hardwoods to Post 10, reached at **Mile 7** via the longer route. A short spur here heads left to an overlook that offers a panoramic view of Grass Lake, the Pigeon River valley and distant hills.

The pathway continues winding a short distance through the upland hardwoods to Post 11. This is the junction where the High Country Pathway continues to the right. The Shingle Mill Pathway heads left and begins a long, sweeping downhill run past the Devil's Soup Bowl, a sinkhole lake. Once you reach the bottom, the trail flattens out for the next couple of miles as you roll past first Grass Lake then scenic little Ford Lake.

Shortly after passing Ford Lake, the trail climbs quickly and merges with the 6-mile loop at **Mile 9**, entering from the left. The trail passes through some old clear-cut areas before crossing Ford Lake Road, and proceeds to roll up and down a small ridge winding along the river. There is small swamp area that you have to cross shortly before reaching Sturgeon Valley Road. It's best to walk your bike through this fragile area.

Manistee National Forest Region

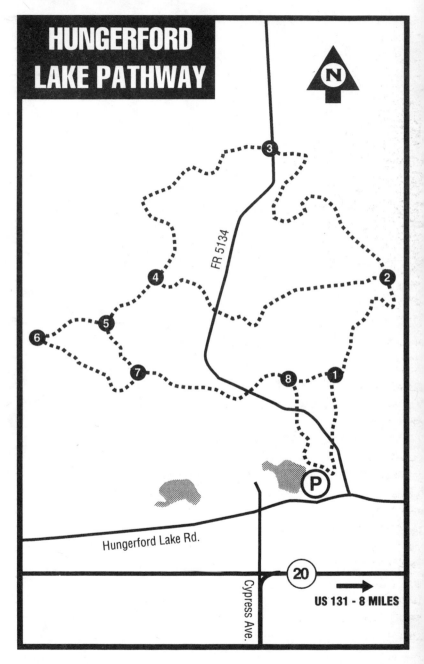

HUNGERFORD LAKE PATHWAY

Hungerford Lake Recreation Area

County: Newaygo
Total Mileage: 13 miles
Terrain: Wooded, rolling hills with a few clear-cut areas and an occasional meadow.
Fees: None
Difficulty: Easy to mostly moderate

Located in the Huron-Manistee National Forest, Hungerford Lake Recreation Area offers a trail system that rolls through beautiful oak-covered hills surrounding the picturesque lake. It's a multiple-use area accommodating a variety of recreational pursuits. Unfortunately horseback riding is one of the permitted uses and has caused a lot of wear and tear on the trail. Bike shops in nearby Big Rapids say the best riding is in early spring and late fall. Most of the horseback riding is done during the summer months.

The trail is somewhat rutted and sandy in spots, but overall offers a nice mix of single and double-track trails. Tucked mostly in the hardwoods that abound in this area, it occasionally crosses a clear-cut area or an old forest meadow.

With a map it's easy to tailor your ride to about any distance you want by using the

97

cross over spurs or the numerous forest roads that intersect this 13-mile system. Near the end of the ride the trail passes close to Hungerford Lake, where primitive campsites are located. Camping is permitted just about anywhere in the recreation area.

Getting There: The trailhead is located just west of Big Rapids. Head west on M-20 for 8.5 miles, or 5 miles if you exit from US-131, to Norwich Town Hall. Head north on Cypress Avenue for a half mile to a cemetery, turn right and continue around Hungerford Lake on Forest Road 5134 to the trailhead on the left. The trailhead is less than a mile from the cemetery.

Information: Contact the White Cloud Ranger District, at 12 N. Charles St., White Cloud, MI 49349; ☎ (616) 689-6696. The district office maintains an information room that is open 24 hours.

Hungerford Trail

Distance: 10 miles
Trail: Single track and double track
Direction: Counter clockwise

You can't see the lake from the trailhead. The trail exits north (right) from the parking area and almost immediately crosses the Forest Road 5134. It continues to climb on a sandy two-track for the first half mile and passes a couple of unmarked spurs. The main trail, however, is well marked with blue diamonds on trees. This section can be very choppy if recently ridden by equestrians.

You reach the first intersection at **Mile 0.8**. If you want to do just a couple of miles, turn left and return to the parking lot for a ride slightly under 2 miles. Go right to continue on the main trail and follow it for an easy mile to Post 2. The trail is again a combination of gently rolling single and two-track. The trail forks twice with a couple of old two-tracks but stay right each time to stay on the main route.

At Post 2, a left will take you across a hilly 1.7-mile section of

The trail system in Hungerford Lake Recreation Area is a mix of single track and double track through forests, clear-cut areas and some open meadows.

trail that rejoins the main loop at intersection 4. It shaves 2.4 miles off the 10 mile ride. Continue right for the long loop. This section is 2.4 miles long and relatively flat until just before Post 3.

The trail immediately drops into a stand of pine, crossing a dirt road where it continues to follow an old two-track. After passing under a set of powerlines, you turn briefly onto a single-track to wind through an area lightly forested in pines.

Shortly the trail will merge briefly with Forest Road 5465. Turn left here, ride just a few yards and turn right onto some single-track that joins another two-track. Turn right on the two-track, which descends, crosses the same forest road and then proceeds to climb steadily. After topping out, the trail exits left as a single-track. Within a short distance the trail crosses Forest Road 5134 and comes to Post 3 at *Mile 4*.

The next couple of miles; short, quick climbs followed by long downhill runs with a few tight turns thrown in, is my favorite portion of the trail. The first mile rolls gently downhill where you intersect a two-track. Turn left and immediately start looking for the trail to exit on the right. It's hard to see, and not well marked in this section. A sharp uphill is followed by another long, fun downhill to another two-track crossing.

The trail merges with another two-track and skirts the edge of a marsh. It takes off to the right as a single-track around a marshy area and climbs a short steep hill before arriving at Post 4, at *Mile 5.8*. It's just a quick downhill through the woods to Post 5.

You can shave about a mile and a couple of hills by taking the left fork at this junction. This spur is fairly easy riding as the trail rolls though a couple of clearings on a combination of double track and single track before rejoining the outer loop at Post 7.

Head up the right fork for the main trail which climbs and drops over a couple of challenging hills before leveling out to Post 6, reached at *Mile 7*.

The trail, which exits left, follows a fairly flat two-track, switching to a single-track before arriving at Post 7 at *Mile 8*. The single track rolls up and down a pine covered ridge as you start the 1.3-mile segment over to Post 8. After descending the ridge the trail flattens out crossing several two-tracks before gently climbing through some hardwoods to Post 8.

The last mile the trail drops sharply off a wooded ridge to cross Forest Road 5134 once more. From here you climb another sandy ridge and descend to Hungerford Lake near the campground. It's just a short climb back to the parking lot from the lake.

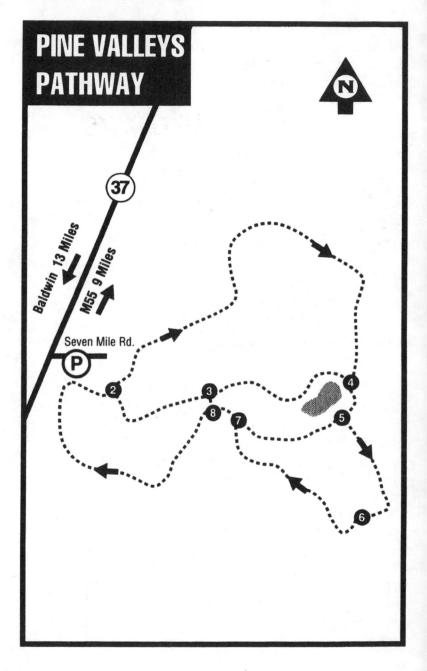

PINE VALLEYS PATHWAY

N

37

Baldwin 13 Miles

M55 9 Miles

Seven Mile Rd.

P

2

3

8

7

4

5

6

Pine Valleys Pathway

County: Lake
Total Mileage: 8 miles
Terrain: Rolling forested hills, Lost Lake, clear cut areas
Fees: None
Difficulty: Easy to moderate

Located in the Pere Marquette State Forest, Pine Valleys Pathway offers a nice combination of single and two-track trails that meander through low hills. The pathway is not a long ride, 6 miles around the outer edge, but it's perfect for anybody looking to make that move from dirt roads to riding wooded trails systems on a mountain bike. The constantly changing landscape offers a nice variety of beautiful pine stands, hardwood forests and open meadows.

The 8-mile system is divided into four loops with the shortest being almost 2 miles and the longest 6 miles. The most scenic sections are around Lost Lake, where there is a walk-in/ride-in campground. In the southern half, the trails wind through clearcuts and areas of rejuvenated forests.

Getting There: The trailhead is just off M-37 about 9 miles south of M-55 or 13 miles north of Baldwin. The trail sign along M-37 directs you east on 7 Mile Road where it's a quarter mile to the trailhead and parking area.

Information: Contact the Baldwin DNR Field Office, P.O. Box 2810, Baldwin, MI 49304; ☎ (616) 745-4651.

Pine Valleys Pathway

Distance: 6.1 miles
Trail: Single track
Direction: Clockwise

The trail takes off from the south end of the parking lot. Traveling in a clock-wise direction, it quickly arrives at Posts 1 and 2...all within a quarter mile. Proceed left at Post 2 for Post 4.

The section between Posts 2 and 4 is the longest single portion of trail at 2.3 miles. After crossing 7 Mile Road, the trail begins a long, gradual climb for about a mile. Once you crest the hill, the trail meanders up and down the wooded ridge line crossing an unmarked two-track at *Mile 1.7*. The trail stays in the short hills and the hardwood forest until it recrosses 7 Mile Road and reaches Post 4 at *Mile 2.5*.

Head towards Post 3 for the best views of Lost Lake or to reach the backcountry campsites on its southwest corner. Proceed straight ahead along a ridge above Lost Lake for Post 5, reached at *Mile 2.7*.

At this junction you can shave a mile off the trip by following the pathway to the west (right), but you'll miss some excellent riding on the way to Post 6.

This segment continues to follow a ridgeline above a series of deep sinkholes, making for a very interesting area geographically. At Post 6, reached at *Mile 3.4*, you cross a two-track that heads down to the sinkholes and Steward Lake.

From the two-track, the trail begins a long, gentle downhill run through a recent clear-cut area. The trail continues through the hardwood forest as it drops into a steep, wooded ravine and back up the other side. After cruising through some more pit-like areas, the trail drops quickly to rejoin the shorter version at Post 7 at **Mile 4.4**.

It's just a short hop over to Post 8 and then another 1.5 miles back to the parking lot. As you leave Post 8, the trail rolls down through a valley and by Little Seyers Lake, a scenic beaver pond. The rest of this segment winds through some thick underbrush before emerging in an open area where the trail disappears. Continue across the open area, and you'll find the trail in some sparse woods on the other side. It's just a short ride to the parking lot from here.

MACKENZIE TRAIL

38 Road

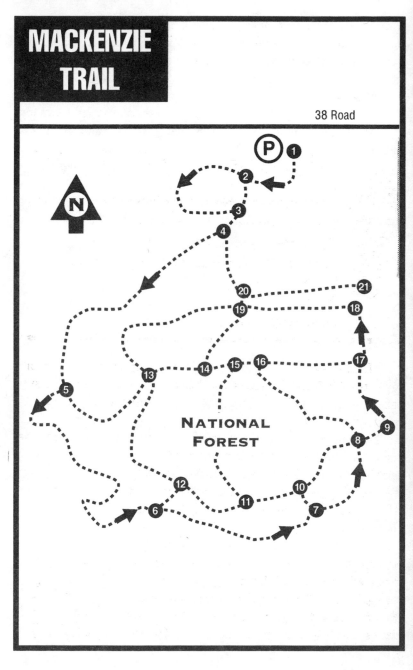

NATIONAL FOREST

MacKenzie Trail

County: Wexford
Total Mileage: 10.8 miles
Terrain: Heavily wooded, rolling hills with a few meadows
Fees: None
Difficulty: Easy

Tucked away among the hills in this region of the Huron-Manistee National Forest, is the MacKenzie Trail, a 11-mile system that, despite the rugged terrain, offers some surprising easy routes for mountain bikers.

Just the drive to the trailhead is spectacular in the fall. The area reminds me of Ohio's southern hill region, which has been dubbed "The Little Smokies." Heading south from Harrietta, there is a stunning overlook (marked platform) just west of Old State Road as you crest the tall range of hills. You can see the Manistee River valley 20 miles away.

Best known as a destination for cross country skiers, the MacKenzie Trail is a mishmash of loops and spurs and, for the most part, easy riding. Those tall hills may be all around you but the trail itself has only a couple of moderate climbs, making it an excellent choice for the

less experienced rider.

Designed for Nordic skiers, the system basically offers a 3.6-mile Inner Loop of easy trail segments and a 5-mile Outer Loop of more and most difficult segments. A handful of spurs connect the two loop. Most of the trail is located among the beautiful hardwoods that dominate the Huron-Manistee National Forest. A few stretches meander across open woodland meadows.

Getting There: From the M-55 and M-115 junction near Cadillac, head west on M-55 for 13 miles and then turn north on Caberfae Road. Within a mile you pass Caberfae Ski Area and then signs for the trail system direct you west on 38 Road. Follow the dirt road for a mile to the posted trailhead on the south side.

Information: You pass the Cadillac Ranger District Office for the Huron-Manistee National Forest on M-55 on the way to the trailhead. The office (☎ 616-775-8539) is open Monday through Friday from 8 a.m. to 5 p.m.

Outer Loop

Distance: 5 miles
Trail: Single track
Direction: Counter clockwise

From the parking lot the trail heads into a pine plantation to Post 2. Take the right loop. It's a nice, easy half-mile ride through the hardwoods over to Post 3. You can take the shorter more direct way on the return.

At Post 3 you descend to a bridge spanning a dry creek bed, then head right where you are faced with one of the few hills in the system. Don't sweat; it's a short hill. You top off at Post 4, where you stay right. The next mile is one of the most scenic sections of the trail. You meander along a ridge that overlooks Johnson Creek along the valley floor and the steep hills on the other side before reaching Post 5 at *Mile 1.7*.

Head right again from this post as the trail gently descends to the creek bank. It's a great place to pause and, if you're quiet, spot deer. From the creek, it's a long, gentle climb to Post 6, reached at **Mile 2.8**.

The ride from Post 6 to Post 8 is an uneventful, easy mile. From Post 8 the Outer Loop continues with an easy, 0.3-mile ride to Post 17 but at this point I like to head inland over to Post 16 then cut back to Post 17. It's a half mile longer but a whole lot more fun with some nice downhill sections and tight turns.

You can head on back via Post 18-19-20 for an easy ride or Post 18-21-20 for a more rolling route. If you can make sense of how they established what posts got what numbers, it's more than I can do. I think they may have used the dart system.

At Post 20, it's a straight, fast downhill run to Post 4, where you're less than a half-mile from the trailhead. Or, you can head back out and add some more sections. There's still some great riding left on some of the inner loops although you've already done most of the strenuous sections.

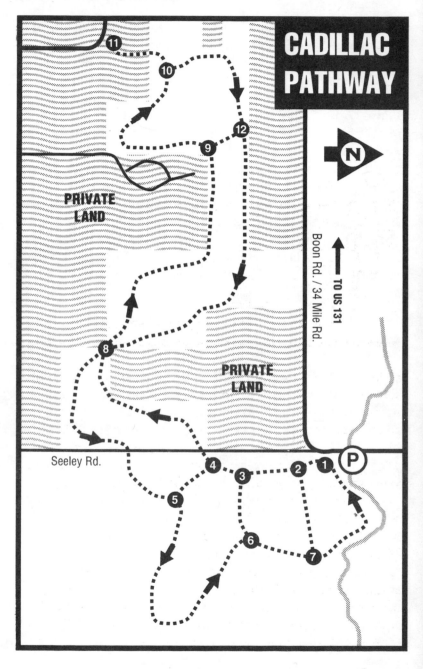

CADILLAC PATHWAY

N

TO US 131

Boon Rd. / 34 Mile Rd.

PRIVATE LAND

PRIVATE LAND

Seeley Rd.

P

Cadillac Pathway

County: Wexford
Total Mileage: 11 miles
Terrain: Rolling, hardwood covered hills and open fields.
Fees: Donation
Difficulty Level: Easy to strenuous

Less than two miles from US-131 and the nearest McDonald's, Cadillac Pathway is about as close to town as you'll get on a northern Michigan trail. Yet the pathway is a pleasant escape from all the tourists and bustle of Cadillac in the summer. Rolling over the small hills that dominate the region, the trail is a classic. It offers everything from easy to strenuous in five different loops, which makes it a great trail for accommodating families and groups.

Most of the trail travels through northern hardwoods while a portion of it meanders along the scenic Clam River. A popular pathway with local mountain bike riders, members from the Michigan Mountain Biking Association northern chapter rolled up their sleeves in 1995 to give the entire system a much needed face lift. Huge piles of trash were removed from the area, new directional posts, benches and trail junction maps were built

and erosion mats were installed.

Basically Cadillac Pathway is a figure-eight system with the eastern half offering the easiest loops and rides. The west half, Post 8 through 12, are the more challenging segments with the steepest hills.

Getting There: The pathway is located just north of Cadillac, almost in the city limits. The main trailhead is reached from US-131 by heading east on Boon Road east for 3.5 miles.

Information: Contact the Cadillac DNR District office, Rte. 1, 8015 South US-131, Cadillac, MI 49601; ☎ (616) 775-9727.

Cadillac Pathway

Distance: 10 miles
Trail: Single track
Direction: Counter clockwise

The pathway starts off gently through a pine plantation and in a little more than half mile you reach Post 4. This is where the trail really starts to roll as you head west. If you wish to avoid the bigger hills, or just looking for a short ride, head over to post 5 at this point to loop back to the trailhead. This would make for an easy 3.5-mile ride that skirts Clam River at the end.

From Post 4, the trail passes within sight of a home and then crosses Seeley Road where caution has to be used crossing the dirt road. Post 8 is reached at **Mile 1.5** and there you'll find a bench after a moderately long climb. Post 8 is the middle of the pathway's figure eight and to the west is a 4.3-mile loop that is much more challenging than what you have just ridden.

Watch for loose sand as you head downhill towards post 9. After rolling over the first couple of hills the ride settles down into a nice rhythm for the next half mile. A long downhill into a narrow valley across a two-track is followed by a fairly steep climb up the other side. You then cross behind some houses and reach Post 9 at **Mile 2.8**.

The next 1.4 miles from Post 9 to Post 12 is a fun section of quick rollers and long, flowing downhills. You cross several two tracks and a pipeline twice. After crossing the pipeline the first time the trail drops down a long grade, levels out and climbs sharply just before reaching Post 10.

The trail leading over to post 11 is a spur that connects with another trailhead just off the parking lot of the Wexford-Missaukee Intermediate School District office on 13th Street, just east of US-131. Head right and enjoy a great 0.7 mile of riding. It's a fun section to accelerate on as the trail drops repeatedly through towering hardwood trees and fragrant pine stands. A long downhill grade leads you past Post 12, located in a stand of red pine at **Mile 4.2**.

The next leg back to Post 8 is a tough ride characterized by long up and down grades. The uphills are wearing while a steep downhill leads into a valley crisscrossed by sandy two-tracks. Head straight across and into the tight trees on the other side. A long, tough uphill leads you back to post 8 at **Mile 5.8**.

Take the right fork to head over to Post 5. This also is a fun section to ride. A firm trail offers some nice long downhills and flats to accelerate through. Cross another two-track and Seeley Road again. A couple of more low hills leads you into post 5 near **Mile 7**.

The 1.4-mile segment to Post 6 passes through some clear-cut areas and along an open ridge offering some nice views of the surrounding hills and valleys. As you head back into the woods, the trail begins a long, slight downhill grade as it rolls into the junction...more fun riding.

It's 1.2 miles back to the trailhead with the rest of the ride being flat and easy. The final segment between Post 7 and the parking lot is a pretty section that skirts the scenic Clam River, a much better spot for a snack or lunch than the local fast food restaurants in town.

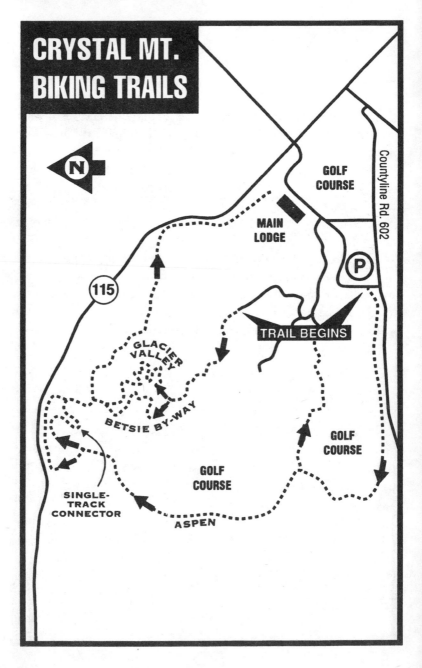

CRYSTAL MT. BIKING TRAILS

N

GOLF COURSE

Countyline Rd. 602

MAIN LODGE

115

P

GLACIER VALLEY

TRAIL BEGINS

BETSIE BY-WAY

SINGLE-TRACK CONNECTOR

GOLF COURSE

GOLF COURSE

ASPEN

Crystal Mountain Resort

County: Benzie
Total Mileage: 11 miles
Terrain: Open resort land along golf course and wooded hills and valleys.
Fees: Trail fee
Difficulty: Easy to strenuous

Located in the Betsie River Valley among the Buck Hills, Crystal Mountain Resort lies in a beautiful area. Hardwood forests, pine stands and flower-laden meadows provide cover for a variety of wildlife with turkey and deer being the most prominent.

Crystal is a full service resort offering a wide variety of activities including mountain biking along with a variety of lodging, an upscale restaurant and bicycles for overnight guests to rent.

You don't need to reserve a room, however, to enjoy the resort's 11-mile system of mountain biking trails. The network is divided into three loops, ranging from the easy, 4.5-mile Aspen Trail around the perimeter of the mountain to the most difficult Glacier Valley, a 3.4-mile loop that features very steep terrain and tight curves. You can even access the Betsie Pathway from the resort.

Getting There: The entrance is off M-115

west of Thompsonville or 28 miles southwest of Traverse City.

Information: Call the resort at ☎ (800) 968-7686 for additional information on vacation packages or to reserve accommodations. Or write Crystal Mountain Resort, 12500 Crystal Mountain Dr., Thompsonville, MI 49683-9742.

Aspen Trail

Distance: 4.5 miles
Trail: Mostly double track
Direction: Clockwise

The Aspen Trail is a great ride for those looking for a little workout yet nothing strenuous. The trail is mostly flat as it winds around the perimeter of the ski hill but you will pick up some small hills along the Betsie By Way on the return.

The ride begins by following the paved road south from the lodge area. The road winds around a housing development and the golf course. Where the road turns sharply southeast heading towards County Line Road, the trail departs to the right. Aspen Trail is mostly two-track with a little single-track near M-115.

The trail parallels County Line Road and the golf course for over a half mile and then reaches a fork shortly after it swings away from the road at **Mile 1.5**. The right fork is a quick shortcut back to the main lodge. Head left to stay on Aspen Trail as it continues to skirt the golf course. For obvious reasons, stay on the bike trail, never stray onto the fairways.

Before **Mile 2**, the connector spur with the Betsie River Pathway departs west from the trail, providing bikers the opportunity to ride this easy pathway and add another 6 miles.

Aspen continues straight ahead. At **Mile 2.8** a challenging single-track continues up and over a small ridge to connect with the Betsie By Way. The easiest way is to continue left as this trail cuts over and parallels M-115 for a short distance then darts back into the woods to join the by way. The final mile includes some small hills before emerging at the main lodge.

Betsie By Way

Distance: 3.1 miles
Trail: Single track
Direction: Clockwise

The Betsie By Way is a roller coaster trail that's constantly changing with climbs, downhill runs and tight corners. The terrain takes some effort and is rated moderate in difficulty.

Just past the pro shop, heading south, turn right on Mountain Center Road. Follow it to Mountain Side Road, where at the end is the trailhead. The trail immediately climbs into the wooded hills above the golf course for an up-and-down ride.

Within a half mile you reach the junction with the rugged Glacier Valley Trail, which departs to the right. At **Mile 1.5** the two trails merge together again and just down the hill is where the Aspen Trail joins for the 1.5-mile ride back to the lodge

Glacier Valley Loop

Distance: 3.4 miles
Trail: Single track
Direction: Clockwise

Glacier Valley is one of the most rugged trails in the Lower Peninsula. It's a strenuous ride that features big hills with heart-pounding climbs and screaming downhill runs. Along the way you can pause and catch your breath at a couple of scenic overlooks of the Betsie River valley and distant Buck Hills.

Immediately after entering Glacier Valley at **Mile 1** of the Betsie By Way, it begins a steep climb for the next half mile. At the top there's a picnic table and great view. Take a breather as the next mile doesn't get any easier. Three fast downhills are followed by three strenuous uphills. At the bottom of each downhill is sharp turn and then a strenuous uphill. Watch your speed here.

The total distance across the hilly interior is only about 1.5 miles before if rejoins the Betsie By Way, but it feels a lot longer. The hardwoods here makes this a beautiful fall ride.

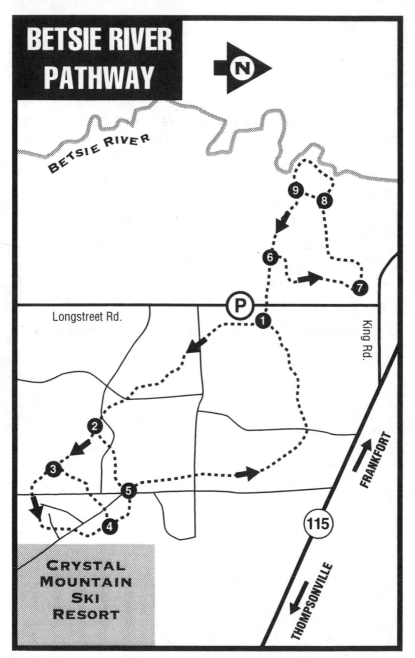

BETSIE RIVER
PATHWAY

BETSIE RIVER

Longstreet Rd.

King Rd.

FRANKFORT

115

THOMPSONVILLE

CRYSTAL
MOUNTAIN
SKI
RESORT

Betsie River Pathway

County: Benzie
Total Mileage: 7 miles
Terrain: Mostly flat with a couple of moderate hills down by the river.
Fees: None
Difficulty: Easy

The riding may be easy, but don't underrate the Betsie River Pathway. It's a beautiful area of constantly changing cover from hardwoods to thick pine stands to open meadows. There's even an old abandoned orchard. The area abounds with wildlife. It's a great area for spotting deer, turkey and ruffed grouse.

It's also a great ride for those who want to ease into "wilderness" mountain biking. It really isn't a wilderness, but the remote and isolated nature of the area is felt out on the trail. Although relatively flat, the single-track trail darts in and around the trees offering a slight technical taste to the ride.

Longstreet Road divides the trail system. It's a 4.4-mile loop on the east side of the road and a 2.7-miles loop to the Betsie River on the west side. The pathway also joins the Crystal Mountain trail system via a short unmarked trail, used infrequently by the resort's guests. The spur is

approximately 0.2 mile south of Post 4. Crystal makes a great lunch spot. It's a little over a mile to the main lodge via the resort's trails. They have some trails for those seeking an aerobic challenge of big hills.

Directions: Follow M-115 2 miles west of the Crystal Mountain entrance and then turn left (south) on King Road. Within a half mile turn left again on Longstreet Road. It's less than a mile to the trailhead on the east side of the road.

Information: Contact the Cadillac DNR District Office, Rte. 1, 8015 South US-131, Cadillac, MI 49601; ☎ (616) 775-9727.

Crystal Moutain Loop

Distance: 4.4 miles
Trail: Single and double track
Direction: Counter clockwise

This is a great ride for novice mountain bikers. The single-track pathway heads south along the wood line and quickly enters the young hardwood forest. For the next mile the trail snakes through the young forest offering some tight, quick turns. Accelerating through this section adds some excitement to the ride despite the flatness of the trail.

Post 2 is at the edge of an old apple orchard. Head right along the edge of the forest. Quickly you head back into the woods and arrive at Post 3 at *Mile 1.5*. Again head right as the trail continues to gently roll though a second-growth forest. Soon you start crossing some open areas and two-tracks. As you enter a stand of pines the trail becomes a two-track for about a mile. At *Mile 1.6*, or slightly before Post 4, a two-track exits to the right. This is the unmarked spur to Crystal's trails. It's not easy to find because of the many two-tracks that criss-cross this area. If you go more than a half-mile before connecting with Crystal, you've chosen the wrong two-track.

It's a half mile to post 5 on a flat single-track. Heading right,

A mountain bikers enjoys the Betsie River Pathway, which connects to the trails at Crystal Mountain Resort to form an 18-mile system for bikers. (photo courtesy of Crystal Mountain Resort)

the trail winds through some more woods and pines before entering a large meadow area. The trail turns into a two-track heading along the edge of the meadow towards a pine stand. Watch closely, because shortly before reaching Post 1 and the parking lot, the trail takes off to the left as a single-track through the woods. It's hard to see, but it takes place at about **Mile 4.2** into the ride...just a quarter mile before the end of the ride on this side of the road.

River Loop

Distance: 2.7 miles
Track: Single and double track
Directon: Counter clockwise

To continue the ride on the River Loop, cross Longstreet Road and ride the short, flat segment to Post 6. This trail on the west side of the road tends to roll a little more. It's nothing a novice can't handle, but you might have to walk up the hill from the river.

Continue right through the old orchard. The trail crosses a couple of two-tracks before reaching post 7 at **Mile 0.9**. The 0.7-mile section between Posts 7 and 8 offers some of the best riding on the pathway. Quickly the trail enters a beautiful, mature hardwood forest and starts a long, downhill descent to the Betsie River. The grade is perfect for letting it coast and enjoying the ride as you sweep through the big trees in long S-like turns.

At Post 8, go left to avoid the final downhill plunge to the river staying along the ridge, or go right to reach the river bank. It's just a short loop, but worth it for a view of the scenic Betsie; a great spot for a lunch or snack break.

The climb out of the river basin to Post 9 isn't bad. It's quick. It's about a mile back to the parking lot. The trail rolls through the woods to Post 6, and returns via the "old orchard" route you rode in on.

Grand Traverse Region

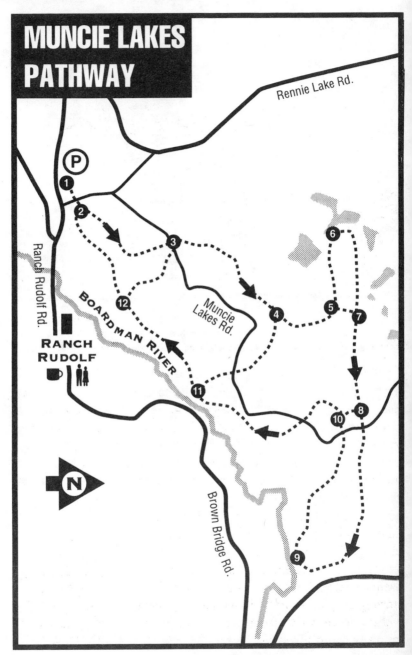

MUNCIE LAKES PATHWAY

Rennie Lake Rd.

P

1

2

3

12

4

5

6

7

8

9

10

11

Muncie Lakes Rd.

BOARDMAN RIVER

Ranch Rudolf Rd.

RANCH RUDOLF

Brown Bridge Rd.

N

Muncie Lakes Pathway

County: Grand Traverse
Total Mileage: 9.8 miles
Terrain: Rolling forest with woodland meadows and clear-cut areas
Fees: Donation
Difficulty: Easy to moderate. Strenuous on river loop

Muncie Lakes Pathway is a beautiful single-track trail. The rolling terrain is perfect for biking with a mixture of hardwoods, pines and upland meadows. Segments of the trail wind past pristine small lakes, over ridges with overlooks of the Boardman River valley or skirt the banks of the swift flowing river.

With all of that going for it why isn't the trail popular with mountain bikers? In a word...horses. In the past, equestrians had completely taken over the trail system. The DNR has made a concentrated effort to redirect the horse traffic in recent years, and has been pretty successful. To credit of the staff at Ranch Rudolf, a nearby riding stable and rustic resort, they have helped educate area equestrians about staying on proper trails. Hopefully the riding will improve on this pathway as more and more bikers discover it.

Muncie Lakes Pathway totals almost 10 miles of trail with several cross over spurs. Most of the system is easy to moderate in difficulty but the segments along the Boardman River, which include several big hills, can be strenuous at times.

Also be prepared for numerous sandy stretches as well as the riding pass clear cuts and other openings for pipe lines and electric powerlines and forest roads. Still the scenery along the Boardman River and Muncie Lakes makes this trail well worth the effort. At the end you can follow a spur to Ranch Rudolf, a popular watering hole after a ride because its trails connect with the Muncie Lakes system.

Getting There: The area is 13 miles southeast of Traverse City. From M-72, turn south on County Road 605 (Williamsburg Road) and follow it for 6 miles until it merges with Supply Road. Continue south on Supply Road until it crosses the Boardman River and then turn west (right) on Brown Bridge Road. Within 2 miles, the road crosses the Boardman again, passes the entrance of Ranch Rudolf and comes to a V-junction. Head right on Ranch Rudolf Road up the steep hill to the posted trailhead on the north side of the road.

Information: Contact the Kalkaska DNR Field Office, M-72, Kalkaska, MI 49646; ☎ (616) 258-2711.

Muncie Lakes Pathway
Distance: 8.7 miles
Trail: Single track
Direction: Clockwise

From the trailhead off Ranch Rudolf Road, the trail skirts the edge of a meadow and a recent clear-cut and reaches Post 3 just before **Mile 1**. Cross Muncie Lakes Road here and continue on the other side. The trail leading right is a cross over spur to Post 12 and Ranch Rudolf.

The main trail continues to head north, providing you with

some nice downhill runs as well as a sandy uphill climb. Right before Post 4, reached at *Mile 1.6*, is a fast and fun downhill run. At the junction, the trail to the right cuts through a large clear-cut area to Post 11 for a 4-mile loop back to the trailhead.

The left fork continues on to Post 5 by climbing a moderate hill, skirting a meadow and climbing another hill. You then plunge down to Post 5, reached just across another dirt road at *Mile 2*. There is occasionally traffic on this road, so look before flying across.

The next mile is the lake section of the ride as you actually pedal along the shore of Muncie Lakes. Head west (left) to Post 6 as the trail climbs a hill through another clear-cut. Be careful of the fast downhill to Post 6 at the edge of the lake where there's normally a lot of loose sand at the bottom. A vault toilet is located here because hunters and fishermen often launch their boats at Post 6.

From the lake the main trail cuts up over the hill, but an old, frequently used trail meanders right along the shore at the base of the hill. If the water isn't too high I prefer riding this scenic way. The trail continues along the shore before heading back up the hill into the woods and Post 7.

It's an easy half-mile through the woods to post 8, reached at *Mile 3.6*. If you want to avoid the hilly, but beautiful, river section head right here for a quick ride to Post 10. The 1.3-mile segment between Posts 8 and 9 is the gem of the system. The single-track crosses Muncie Lakes Road again and a snowmobile trail and then plunges down into a deep little valley. You quickly climb the other side to crest a hill and cross a couple snowmobile trails.

This is where the ride starts to get fun as the trail winds through alternating woods and meadows. It swings right after entering the woods again and descends to cross another two-track. The trail then proceeds for a half mile along a ridge that drops in a series of levels to Post 9 at the edge of the Boardman River, reached near *Mile 5*. Be careful of the last plunge, a steep slope that includes two huge pine trees guarding the trail at the

Trilliums fill the woods tthroughout the Grand Traverse Region and much of Northern Michigan, blooming from mid-May through early June.

bottom like goal posts.

Post 9, roughly the halfway point of the ride, is a great spot to enjoy the scenic beauty of the area and rest. The next mile is mostly uphill. The trail is not steep, but composed of long tiring grades. You will finally crest the ridge at a power line, which the trail crosses, and then begin another long descent. The trail swings left at the bottom and begins another steep climb. Soon after crossing Muncie Lakes Road, you reach Post 10 at **Mile 6**.

The last leg of the trail is a 2.7-mile ride through Post 11, Post 12 and then back to Post 2 and the parking lot. From Post 10 the trail descends to cross a snowmobile route, crests a little knoll on the other side and crosses Muncie Lakes Road for the third and final time. As you drop down another little dip along side a clear-cut, check out the view from the ridge directly in front of you before heading back into the woods. It offers a panoramic view of the Boardman River and valley.

You have one more good climb after crossing the snowmobile path again before arriving at Post 11, reached at **Mile 7**. The rest of the ride is fairly easy to slightly rolling. A left at Post 12 would take you down to Ranch Rudolf in less than a quarter mile. But be prepared because the spur to the resort is sandy.

I've also found that the numerous two-tracks and snowmobile trails that crisscross the area are too sandy for a good ride. The area attracts a lot of four-wheel traffic, which keeps the terrain pretty chewed up.

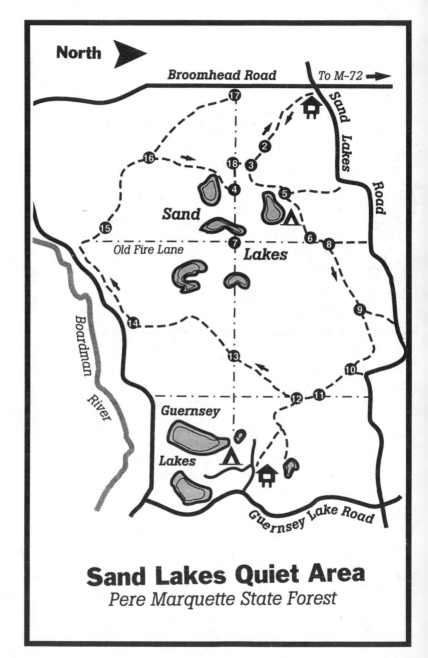

Sand Lakes Quiet Area
Pere Marquette State Forest

Sand Lakes Quiet Area

County: Grand Traverse
Total Mileage: 11 miles
Terrain: Gently rolling to hilly forest area, small lakes
Fees: Donation
Difficulty: Easy to moderate

Sand Lakes Quiet Area is a popular trail system year round. The 3,500-acre tract supports a variety of outdoor activities from hiking and backcountry camping to fishing, hunting and skiing.

In recent years, mountain bikers have also discovered the non-motorized tract, located south of Williamsburg and 15 miles east of Traverse City. The pathway is firm and offers some great single-track riding though the heavily forested area. Wildlife is abundant around the small picturesque lakes.

Sand Lakes is an 11-mile trail system which includes a 7.5-mile loop around the perimeter of the tract. The quiet area is also crisscrossed with old fire lanes that appear as overgrown two-tracks while there are all kinds of two tracks and forest roads throughout this portion of the Pere Marquette State Forest. Many offer good riding and are worth checking out. Consult a good atlas, such as the "Michigan Atlas & Gazetteer" from

Delorme Mapping, to locate the numerous forest roads.

There is a rustic state forest campground on the east end of the quiet area, along the shore of Guernsey Lake. Primitive camping is also permitted just about anywhere in the Quiet area, and is popular around the little lakes on the west end which are accessible by bike or foot only.

Getting There: From M-72, 6 miles east of US-31, turn south on Broomhead Road. The trailhead parking lot is reached in 6 miles south on the right side of the dirt road.

Information: Contact the Traverse City DNR Field Office, 404 W. 14th St., Traverse City, MI 49684; ☎ (616) 922-5280.

Sand Lakes Quiet Area

Distance: 7.5 miles
Trail: Single track
Direction: Clockwise

The trail heads straight south from the parking lot and crosses Sand Lakes Road in just a few yards. The single-track then starts to gently descend as it rolls towards Post 2. You continue to drop most of the way to the junction, winding in and out of the trees. A few of the downhills are slightly sandy near the bottom.

Continue straight through Post 2, to climb a slight rise and plunge down the other side to post 3, reached at **Mile 1**. The downhill is tight as it flows through the trees like a slalom course. Head left towards Post 5 and the trail will level out along a ledge above the first of the many little lakes located in the Quiet area.

Post 5 is reached at **Mile 1.3** but take the time to ride the short distance down to the shore of Sand Lake Number One. It's bright waters contrast with the surrounding wooded hillsides to create a scene that is the essence of northern Michigan. There is a vault toilet here and a water pump.

The trail rolls through a mile of great pedal-and-shifting between posts Post 5 and Post 9. Take a quick left at Post 6 and Post

8 is just up the slight grade along an old fire lane. The right fork is the fire lane that heads south 1.5 miles to Post 15 across some of the biggest hills in the system.

The riding just keeps getting better with the half-mile section between Post 9 and Post 10, my favorite portion of the ride. It's a narrow single-track with quick hills and tight turns.

Post 10 is reached at *Mile 2.4* and here you head right again. A left turn at any of these posts up to this point would take you out to Sand Lakes Road. From Post 10 you ride south to the southern border of the Quiet Area. The next 1.8 miles to Post 14 is an easy ride with long gentle grades. The trail heading left at Post 12 leads to Guernsey Lake Road and the state forest campground. It's a mile to the road and less to the campground.

At Post 14, reached at *Mile 4.4*, the Shore-to-Shore horseback trail comes through the area. The two trails used to merge here. Fortunately, the Traverse City DNR Field Office, already fighting horseback traffic at Lost Lake and Muncie Lakes, recognized the trails needed to be separated and did so in 1995.

Head right at Post 14 up the slight grade. The trail follows a ridge above a forest road that forms the southern boundary. The trail here offers some great riding for about a half mile before dropping off the ridge down a sandy rut. Be careful! Head right after coming off the ridge, and Post 15 is just ahead near *Mile 5*.

The next section to Post 16 is somewhat sandy. The junction is reached at *Mile 5.6* and here you head right. The trail comes off a ridge dropping into a pretty little valley and emerges along the shore of Sand Lake Number Three. Ride around the lake and up a slight grade where you'll come to Post 4 at *Mile 6.2*. I don't recommend trying the ride over to Post 17 and back to Post 4. The trail is sandy in spots, often rutted and really poor riding.

At Post 4 head left and roll over a couple of small hills to Post 18 in a short distance. Turn right, and it's another short easy ride back to Post 2. Unfortunately that great downhill ride at the beginning from Post 1 is uphill going the other way. However, it's not a bad ride as the uphill grades aren't steep and the trail is firm.

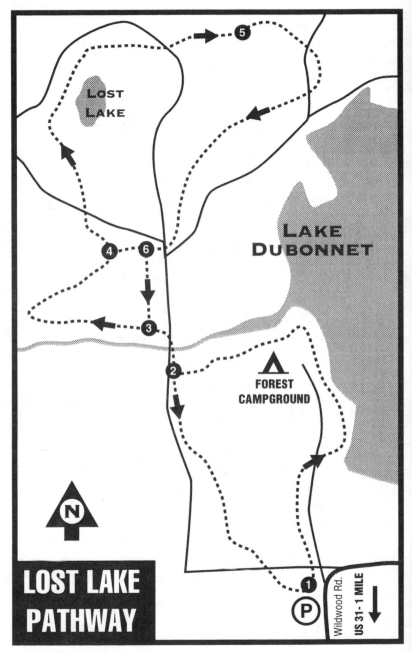

LOST LAKE
PATHWAY

Lost Lake Pathway

County: Grand Traverse
Total Mileage: 6.3 miles
Terrain: Forested, gently rolling hills, Lake Dubonet and the headwaters of the Platte River.
Fees: None
Difficulty: Easy

Lost Lake Pathway is a great place for novice riders, families and groups of varied levels of ability. The terrain is non-threatening and makes for an easy ride for even the most novice mountain biker.

The only thing riders need to keep an eye out for are a few sandy patches and the erosion caused by horseback riders on the outer two loops. The stretches of sand will always be there but hopefully the potmarks in the trail caused by the hoofs and weight of the horses will end as the entire trail system is posted off limits to equestrians.

The terrain is not only easy to ride but interesting. The topography, transitional small sink hole lakes created by glacial debris and melting ice deposits, is typical of how the glaciers formed this region. Lake Dubonnet itself, however, was created in 1956 when a stream was dammed

135

to improve fishing and waterfowl habitat.

A state forest campground, overlooking the Lake Dubonet shoreline, is located on the first loop. Facilities at this 50-site rustic campground include a boat launch, a long fishing pier onto the lake and group sites. Renown Interlochen Arts Academy, the site of frequent music performances in the summer, is only minutes away, so the campground is frequently filled during July and early August.

Getting There: From Traverse City head west on US-31 for 14 miles, or a mile past M-137, and then turn north on Wildwood Road beside Interlochen Golf Course. It's a mile to the trailhead and parking lot.

Information: Contact the Traverse City DNR Field Office, 404 14th St., Traverse City, MI 49684; ☎ (616) 946-4920.

Lost Lake Pathway

Distance: 6.3 miles
Trail: Single track
Direction: Both counter clockwise and clockwise

The first leg through the state forest campground is easy, scenic riding. The single-track trail exits the parking lot to the north and cuts through a hardwood forest, reaching the edge of Lake Dubonnet at **Mile 0.5**. Be careful here as you cross two busy dirt roads that lead to the campground. The trail continues to follow the shoreline for a mile as it winds between the lake and campground before reaching Post 2 at **Mile 1.4**.

Drop down on the two-track and head right across the earthen dam. Post 3 is on the left just across the dam. The next leg meanders along the creek basin, cuts over the small ridge above the creek and descends to Post 4 at **Mile 2.2**. This sandy section has suffered the greatest damage from horse traffic.

Head left at Post 4. The surface of the trail will improve shortly as you start winding around the Lost Lake basin. There was a

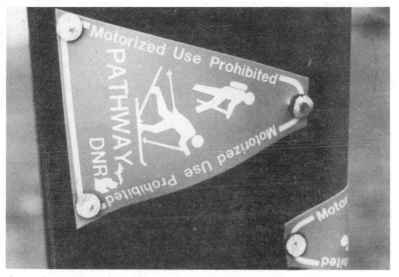

State forest pathways, like the system at Lost Lake, are marked with a variety of blazes, signposts and distinctive blue pathway triangles.

time when this small lake occupied the entire basin. In a few more hundred years it will completely disappear, the fate of many small pit lakes created by the last glacier some 10,000 years ago.

As you depart from Lost Lake, the trail climbs slightly and crosses the dirt road that extends over the dam. Post 5 is reached at **Mile 4** and precedes along large blueberry bog on the right and then cuts through a beautiful stand of large red pines. These trees were planted almost a century ago after most of the area was logged.

The trail continues to climb some small hills and crosses a couple of two-tracks before reaching Post 6 just beyond **Mile 5**. Head left as the pathway skirts the edge of another bog. It's just a short distance to Post 3, where you again cross the dam.

This time head south (right) to return to the parking lot. This last mile is a fun ride. The trail is fast and firm as it meanders though pine and hardwood and across a ridge overlooking Christmas Tree Lake. You cross one dirt road just before **Mile 6** and then quickly reach the parking lot.

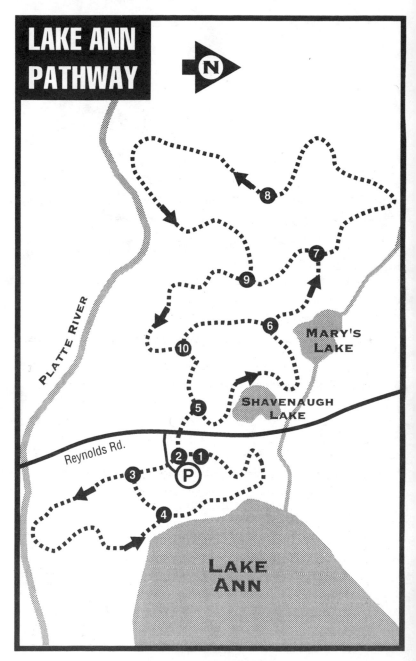

LAKE ANN
PATHWAY

N

PLATTE RIVER

8

9

7

6

MARY'S LAKE

10

5

SHAVENAUGH LAKE

Reynolds Rd.

2 1

P

3

4

LAKE ANN

Lake Ann Pathway

County: Benzie
Total Mileage: 5 miles
Terrain: Moderate hills with a few steep
sections, lakes and the Platte River
Fees: Donation
Difficulty: Easy to strenuous

Just outside the tiny hamlet of LA (Lake Ann that is) sits a compact DNR pathway that has quietly become a favorite of Traverse City riders. Tucked between Lake Ann, the Chain O' Lakes and the Platte River, it offers a challenging, winding ride through the hills surrounding all of this water as well as a short, gentle loop along the lakeshore.

The system is divided by Reynolds Road. To the west the trail winds past three small lakes and then the beautiful, wild Platte River all through majestic hardwood and spruce. This is the bulk of the system and hills you encounter range from rolling to strenuous climbs.

East of Reynolds Road is an easy 1.8-mile loop that passes through the campground and along an undeveloped portion of the Lake Ann shoreline. The trailhead is also located in the rustic campground, which includes a separate

dayuse parking lot, vault toilets and boat launch on the lake.

For a quick, scenic and vigorous ride, Lake Ann Pathway is the best choice in the Traverse City area.

Getting There: From Interlochen head west on US-31 for 5 miles and watch for the DNR ski trail sign. Turn north on Reynolds Road, and in 4 miles is the posted trailhead parking lot on the east side of the road.

Information: Contact the DNR Field Office, 404 W. 14th St., Traverse City, MI 49684; ☎ (616) 922-5280.

East of Reynolds Road

Distance: 1.8 miles
Trail: Single track
Direction: Counter clockwise

This is scenic, easy riding. From the parking lot head south across the entrance road to Post 3. The trail gently drops down to the Platte River and then loops back to Post 4 reached on the shore of Lake Ann near *Mile 1*. Continue north as the trail stays along the shore until it reaches the boat launch. At this point you swing south into some easy hills, pass through the campground and end up back at the parking lot.

West of Reynolds Road

Distance: 3.4 miles
Trail: Single track
Direction: Counter clockwise

This time cross Reynolds Road to post 5 and get ready for a challenge. The 3.4-mile loop on this side of the road contains some good hills.

Head north (right) from Post 5 as the trail descends to wind along the shore of Shavenaugh Lake, named for the first settler who lived here in the early 1800's. The early settler is supposedly buried by one of the towering pines located on the opposite side of the small lake. Shavenaugh Lake is the first of a series of inter-connected lakes referred to locally as the Chain O' Lakes.

The trail enters a roller coaster terrain as it climbs, drops, climbs and drops again along the shore of Mary's Lake. You then begin a long climb to post 6, reached at only **Mile 0.6** of the ride.

Head right for a short, hilly ride over to Post 7, where you stay right again to enter the backside of the loop. If you haven't had enough hills get ready. Some of the biggest and meanest are along the backside, a 1.8-mile stretch to Post 9.

This segment begins with the trail climbing above an unnamed lake and then rolling across a series of hills that seem to grow in size. Be careful of the fast sweeping downhill as you plunge off this ridge line just before passing Post 8 at **Mile 1.8**. At one time the trail use to plunge headlong down this ridge with no turns, making for a exciting ride if you survived it. But after a few acci-dents, the DNR rerouted this stretch. For the most part the trail surface is firm, but you will encounter a couple of sandy sections on the backside of the loop here.

After Post 8 you start to leave the hardwoods behind as you head into lowlying areas along the Platte River. You're riding past a bog or two but the trail remains firm with the exception of a couple of minor "soft" areas. There are also a few good hills in this next segment with steep drops and sharp turns at the bot-tom. Ride under control.

The trail continues to meander along this scenic, wild stretch of the Platte River for a quarter mile. It's a great place to spot deer if you're quiet and alert. It's also just a nice spot to simply relax and enjoy the quiet and beauty of this pristine area. This is what mountain biking is all about...getting to areas like this.

After leaving the Platte, the trail begins to slowly climb out of the river basin back up into the surrounding hills, reaching Post 9 at **Mile 2.7**. The segment to Post 10 is more rolling single track, a fun ride as you accelerate through the drops and turns.

From the last junction at Post 10, it's just a quarter mile back to Post 5 and the parking lot on the east side of Reynolds Road.

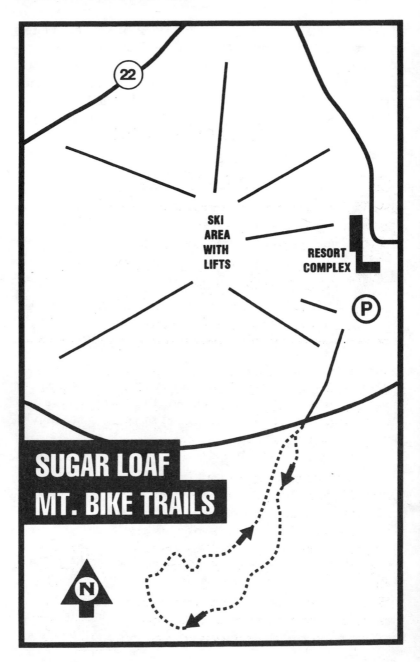

22

SKI
AREA
WITH
LIFTS

RESORT
COMPLEX

P

**SUGAR LOAF
MT. BIKE TRAILS**

N

Sugar Loaf Resort

County: Leelanau
Total Mileage: To be determined
Terrain: Hills, meadows and some sand
Fees: To be determined
Difficulty: In the past it's been difficult because of hills and sandy trails.

Mountain biking at Sugar Loaf Resort was in a state of change as this book went to print. A new golf course was in the process of being built that would include most of the area where the resort's original mountain biking trails were located. Check with the resort for the latest trail map, which should be ready in the spring of 1996.

Located along the sandy western side of Leelanau County, "the Loaf" is a striking contrast of woods, open dune-like areas, grass lands and spectacular views from the summit of the ski hill. It's hosted some major mountain biking events in the past, and there are plans of staging more after the new golf course is finished.

Sugar Loaf offers all the typical amenities of a major northern Michigan resort, including an excellent restaurant and a variety of lodging.

They also rent mountain bikes at the golf shop.

Keep in mind that mountain biking is prohibited on the trails of nearby Sleeping Bear Dunes National Lakeshore. The erosion factor of mountain bikes is far too great to allow the activity on the delicate dunes, especially when so many include large stretches of open sand.

For additional riding opportunities in this section of the Leelanau Peninsula, however, follow the many secondary dirt roads that can easily be reached from the resort. A particularly fun and scenic ride is following Port Oneida Road and Basch Road off M-22 in the Pyramid Point area of the national lakeshore. At Sugar Loaf, the staff can suggest other road routes.

Getting There: Take M-72 west from Traverse City to CR-651, and head north through Cedar. Sugar Loaf is 20 miles northwest of Traverse City and signs will direct you to the resort once you're on CR-651. When passing through Cedar, stop at Pleva's Meats, home of the best meat market in the area. Some of his meat and cherry combinations have received acclaim nationally.

Information: Call Sugar Loaf at ☎ (800) 632-9802 for an unpdate on the trail or reservations.

Double Dipper

Distance: 3 miles
Trail: Single track
Direction: Clockwise

The only thing certain about the new mountain biking trails, is that they will be in the area of the current Double Dipper trail. This 3-mile loop offered some of the best riding at the Loaf and had one of the firmest trail surface.

Double Dipper had always been the gem of the old system. On the rolling trail, you were able to completely escape from the resort. It meandered over hills as well as through hardwood forests and open meadows. You cross over a county road on the way

A mountain biker pauses for a scenic view of the Leelanau Peninsula near Sugar Loaf Resort.

and back

Sugar Loaf has the acreage in area of the Douple Dipper to develop a first class trail system that will offer both diversity and distance. Especially distance as the loop is only 3 miles long and most northern Michigan resorts offer considerably more mileage for bikers to enjoy.

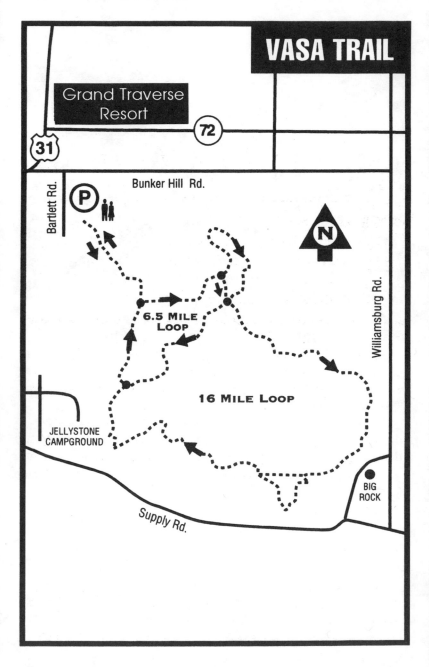

VASA TRAIL

Grand Traverse Resort

72

31

Bartlett Rd.

P

Bunker Hill Rd.

N

Williamsburg Rd.

6.5 MILE LOOP

16 MILE LOOP

JELLYSTONE CAMPGROUND

BIG ROCK

Supply Rd.

VASA Trail

County: Grand Traverse
Total Mileage: 18 miles
Terrain: A hilly, forested area
Fees: Donation
Difficulty: Strenuous

The VASA Trail is one of the premier mountain biking trails in the northern Lower Peninsula, a route that is on a par with the famed Potawatomi Trail in the Pinckney Recreation Area near Ann Arbor in southern Michigan.

It was originally developed to host the North American VASA Race, the second largest cross country ski race in the United States. But the event is only one day a year (second Saturday of February) and the rest of the year this beautiful trail system is open to the public.

The VASA Trail is a state forest pathway, but is overseen and maintained by a local board of volunteers, who also stage the ski race each year.

George Lombard, somewhat of a local legend, is the man responsible for laying out the trail and working with the DNR. Lombard, who is retired, represented the United States at the

World Handicap Winter Olympics in 1984. He races mountain bikes and still cross country skis competitively; all with an artificial leg. He also has been very active working with the DNR to maintain and develop a statewide network of biking trails.

The trail is 16-feet wide in most places. It follows a series of old abandoned forest roads, which were quite sandy in spots. Now after several years of use as a bike path, and the exclusion of ORVs, the trail has solidified nicely. Routine maintenance has also helped.

The VASA Trail is fairly tough riding with some long, steep hills on both the long and short trails. Meandering over the hill and dale country that surrounds the Grand Traverse Bay basin, the trail slices through deep hardwood and stately pine forests. At times you are far from civilization, so prepare accordingly, and let someone know your schedule. This is not a ride for novice bikers.

Getting There: The trailhead is located in the hills above East Bay. From US-31, just south of its intersection with M-72, head east on Bunker Hill Road for a mile to Bartlett Road. Turn right and follow Bartlett Road to the trailhead parking lot.

Information: Contact the North American VASA Office, P.O. Box 581, Traverse City, MI 49685-0581; ☎ (616) 938-4400.

25-Kilometer Loop
Distance: 16 miles
Trail: Single track
Direction: Clockwise
From the parking lot, The trail heads east and in a half mile you cross scenic Acme Creek. At this point you begin climbing for the next mile along some long grades. The trail markers are in kilometers, but we'll stay with miles in this description. Most riders still think of distance in mileage terms rather than kilometers.

After cresting at the top of the first big climb at *Mile 1.3*, the trail drops down to a fork in the trail. Head left, the return trail

Northern Michigan is the site of many biking events that include races for children as a way to introduce them to off-road riding.

is the right fork. The section you just completed is actually an out-and-back spur from the trailhead and you will return via the same trail.

Shortly after crossing the powerline the trail rolls down a long descent, crosses a two-track and climbs back up into the hills on the other side. At **Mile 2.5** the trail forks again. Continue left for the 25 Kilometer Loop, the long ride and right for the 10 Km Loop.

The trail rolls through a great riding section for the next two miles, characterized by quick, steep descents, long, gradual uphills and sections of flowing, S-like turns. Shortly after **Mile 4**, a spur takes off to the right to rejoin the 10 Kilometer Loop just a few yards south of the intersection you passed earlier. This is a way to add a couple of extra miles on the shorter ride.

In less than a half mile the 25 Kilometer Loop drops sharply down a right hand turn into a pit-like valley. Be careful on this descent; it's fast and sometimes sandy. You then climb a couple of short hills and cross another powerline.

The trail enters some deep woods on the other side, and begins to climb steadily for the next mile or so, culminated by the *big climb* of the ride. Known as "The Wall," it's a long, steep sandy hill that seems to go on forever. Enjoy the nice long descents on the other side, you've earned them.

At **Mile 6.3** the trail climbs through a beautiful hardwood forest, crosses an abandoned oil drilling site (slowly being reclaimed by the forest), and flattens out for a couple of miles.

This is a great section to throw it into high gear and just cruise. The trail crosses several two-tracks and forest roads through this section. At **Mile 8.5**, the trail again forks. Cresting the little knoll, the left fork enters "Jack Pine Valley," a series of steep climbs and descents through this deep valley that lasts a little more than a mile. Or you can take the right fork, which is fairly easy riding and rejoin the other trail in a half mile.

The trail remains relatively flat for the next three miles as it passes under another powerline and crosses several two-tracks;

some can be busy with traffic. It's always a good idea to look before crossing.

The longer and shorter trails merge at **Mile 13**. The trail continues to roll through more hardwood forests, crossing more two-tracks and emerges along the edge of a large open valley known as "The Meadows." You're just about home.

One more long, steep climb brings you to the intersection with the spur that takes you back to the parking lot. It's all downhill from here. Be advised that this spur is two-way traffic, watch for bikers and hikers coming up the hill.

10 Kilometer Loop

Distance: 7 miles
Trail: Single track
Direction: Clockwise

The shorter loop follows the same route as the 25 Kilometer Loop until they split at **Mile 2.5**. The 10 Kilometer Loop then meanders along a ridge through a stand of large pine, crosses a powerline and drops down to cross some two-tracks before entering a beech-maple forest. In a short distance the trail swings left, drops down a long, steep hill and proceeds to climb an even longer, steeper grade on the opposite side of the narrow valley.

Reaching the top, the trail emerges from the woods and starts a long, gentle descent through a large clear-cut area. At the bottom is where the two trails merge again.

The total distance across the short-cut spur is 1.5 miles. The rest of the this loop is on the existing VASA Trail that was described above.

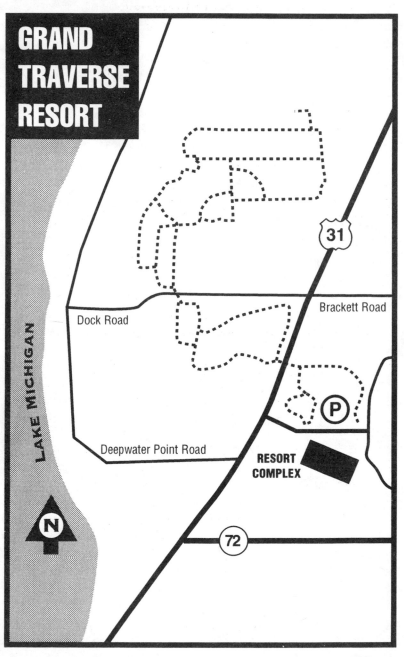

GRAND
TRAVERSE
RESORT

LAKE MICHIGAN

31

Dock Road

Brackett Road

Deepwater Point Road

P

RESORT
COMPLEX

72

N

Grand Traverse Resort

County: Grand Traverse
Total Mileage: 5.6 miles
Terrain: Gently sloping open and wooded terrain
Fees: None presently, but possibly in the future
Difficulty: Easy to slightly moderate

Just by virtue of its size, the Grand Traverse Resort has become one of the most recognized landmarks in Grand Traverse County. Being the only 17-story building north of Detroit, it's certainly hard to miss.

The Resort (as it's called by locals) is a world-class facility. It's played host to the prestigious National Governor's Conference, the World Travel Writers Society and numerous other national and international conferences. A multitude of luxury rooms, suites and condos are available to rent. The complex houses 10 restaurants, a shopping gallery, tennis and racquetball courts and a complete health facility.

In the way of mountain biking, the resort has a 5-mile trail on site that is surprisingly remote and fun to ride, but definitely not hard. Future plans call for connecting the Grand Traverse Resort into the Traverse Area Recreational Trail (TART), which would give guests

access to downtown Traverse City 10 miles away as well as the VASA Trail that lies a mile to the south.

Presently there is no trail fees for riding the pathway but the rental bikes are available only for guests.

Getting There: The resort is 6 miles northeast of Traverse City at the intersection of M-72 and US-31. There is also a trailhead located on US-31, just north of the resort. This starting point eliminates having to cross the busy highway.

Information: Contact the Grand Traverse Resort, P.O. Box 404, Acme, MI 49610-0404; ☎ (800) 748-0303.

Village Pathway

Distance: 5 miles
Trail: Single track
Direction: None

The name is really a misnomer. It has nothing to do with a village, and actually provides a much more remote ride once you cross busy US-31. The ride is fairly easy, but does have some long, gentle uphills that you'll feel by the time you crest the hill.

It's a half mile via the pathway from the resort complex to the US-31 crossing with some of it through a wooded section. After crossing the busy highway, head right. The trail cuts in back of an old house that is used to house Resort workers and then drops into some open meadows to a "T" intersection.

Again, head right. The trail quickly heads into the trees and parallels Dock Road briefly before crossing it. The trails on the other side of the road are all short, but fun rideable sections. They aren't marked for any particular direction. You can add or detract sections as you choose. The combinations are too numerous to describe.

Some of the sections stay along the edge of the woods, some slice through, and some meander across flowered meadows and along cherry orchards. One of the sections cuts right by the Mu-

The Grand Traverse Resort is a world-class facility that offers a limited mountain biking trail system plus easy access to the nearby VASA Trail.

sic House, a popular tourist stop which houses an interesting collection of music memorabilia and historical instruments. At the northern end of the system is a short spur that leads to a picnic table and a partial view of the East Bay of Grand Traverse Bay.

If you follow the outside perimeter of the trails, it's a 5-mile ride. When you cross Dock Road on the return, continue straight ahead through the woods. Within a third of a mile after crossing, look for the trail that heads left and starts to slowly climb back up to the Resort. The spur that continues out into the meadow eventually splits again ending at either a K-Mart store or a church.

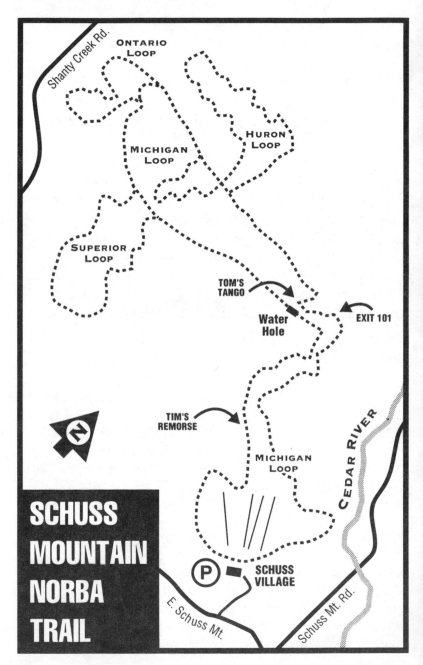

Schuss Mountain NORBA Trail

County: Antrim
Total Mileage: 13 miles
Terrain: Hills, forests and meadows
Fees: Trail pass obtained at Schuss Village
Difficulty: Strenuous

This is the NORBA course that the pro riders tackle each summer when 30,000 spectators and 1500 riders invade the rugged hill and dale country of Antrim County. The event has put northern Michigan on the national mountain biking map.

Shanty Creek, a full service resort with a variety of lodging and restaurants, jumped on the mountain bike racing bandwagon in 1993. It's been a positive experience for Shanty Creek and the success has spurred other Northern Michigan resorts to also cater to mountain bikers. Most now offer bike rentals and trails systems, and several are sponsoring their own racing events.

But, there is only one NORBA course, and it is tough. The trail was designed by local mountain biking guru Tom White with the aid of Bob LaMontaine. It's a challenging ride that climbs the ski hill and continues to roll up and down some big hills. The single-track portions would give a mountain goat trouble, let alone a mountain bike. It's a pretty ride, however, with the

deep forests, mountain meadows and overlooks combining to create a scenic backdrop.

The 13-mile system is divided into four loops, each one named after a Great Lake with the Michigan Loop the longest at 7 miles and Erie Loop the shortest at 0.8 mile. The trails are in a constant state of revision. Sections will be constantly closed and opened for repair and expansion of the resort. It's a good idea to obtain a map from the resort before taking off on your ride. Rental bikes are available for overnight guests.

Getting There: The resort is five miles west of Mancelona off US-131. Follow M-88 west from the light and look for the directional signs to Shanty Creek's Schuss Mountain Village.

Information: For room reservations or more information contact Shanty Creek, Bellaire, MI 49615; ☎ (800) 678-4111.

Michigan Loop

Distance: 7 miles
Trail: Single track and two-track
Direction: Counter clockwise

This is the NORBA, the course the pros will ride five to six times. It's an extremely tough ride by itself while the other four loops all branch off of it so adding mileage is easy.

Much of this loop is through a deep forest. So deep, that the sun seldom shines in here, which means the trail has trouble drying out after heavy rains. Riding is best during dry spells.

The ride starts off with a very tough climb over the top of the ski hill via a series of switch backs. Once you crest the ski hill you have a long, swift ride down a two-track on the other side. It continues to roll up and down some big hills before switching to some tough single track through Exit 101 and Tom's Tango that clings tenaciously to the hillsides.

The ride settles down a little at this point as it heads towards a former hunting preserve called the Game Farm. This is the first meadow-like area you'll encounter. At **Mile 3**, the 2-mile Huron Loop takes off here and reconnects with the Michigan Loop just ahead. The 0.8 mile Erie Loop connection is also in this area.

The ride reenters the woods and rolls through Fiber-Optic, a series of roller coaster-like small hills. It's a fun section once you make it up the first steep climb. At **Mile 3.6** the scenic 1.1-mile Ontario Loop takes off right after this section. You're roughly halfway around at this point.

The Michigan Loop continues up a wooded hill and emerges into a vast meadow. You wind though the meadow and reenter the woods around Frog Holler. The 3-mile Superior Loop takes off at the top of the long hill at **Mile 4.2**.

The Michigan Loop continues to follow an old two-track into a heavily forested area, rolling up and down several challenging hills. It's along this stretch that you'll encounter the infamous "water hole" at **Mile 5.4**. I advise riding around the water-filled pit. It was designed as a risk-taking possibility for race participants to shave a second or two from their time by leaping over the hazard. It's popular with spectators, but the water hole has created a controversy among racers.

More tough single track alternates with two-track as the trail continues to climb and drop until a final long climb up the back side of the ski hill. This climb is called Tim's Remorse, and you will be too. It was named after one of the co-founders of this race, Tim Brick, owner of Brick Wheel bike shop in Traverse City.

Be careful on the way down the face of the ski hill. It's fast and treacherous, but fun if you like speed. Or be thankful that you're not a pro rider. I can't imagine having to do this loop more than once a year.

Huron Loop

Distance: 2 miles
Trail: Single track
Direction: Counter clockwise
The Huron, as well as the other short loops, offers some of

The start of the famed NORBA race, the largest mountain biking event in Michigan.

the best riding. The four are mostly single track, as opposed to the Michigan Loop, which is more old two-track.

The Huron Loop winds through mostly hardwood forest with a few forays into meadowlands. The loop offers lots of hills. It's a microcosm of the main loop, but without the really tough climbs.

Erie Loop

Distance: 0.8 miles
Trail: Single track
Direction: Clockwise

This is a sporty little single track ride. It winds into the hardwoods for a tough climb and then back down. It's classic Tom White trail.

Ontario Loop

Distance: 1.1 miles
Trail: Single track
Direction: Counter clockwise

Once you climb out of the hardwoods, a spectacular view of the Shanty Creek Village, Lake Bellaire and distant hills opens up. The trail winds through a fragrant pine stand and some pretty meadows. It's a great ride. Don't miss it.

Superior Loop

Distance: 2.9 miles
Trail: Single track
Direction: Counter clockwise

This is a pretty ride that alternates between woodlands and meadows. The trail flows nicely with a couple of good climbs and nice long downhill cruising segments such as the section dubbed TMF (Too Much Fun). The name says it all. This section offers more variety in ecosystems than any of the other loops.

Tip of the Mitt Region

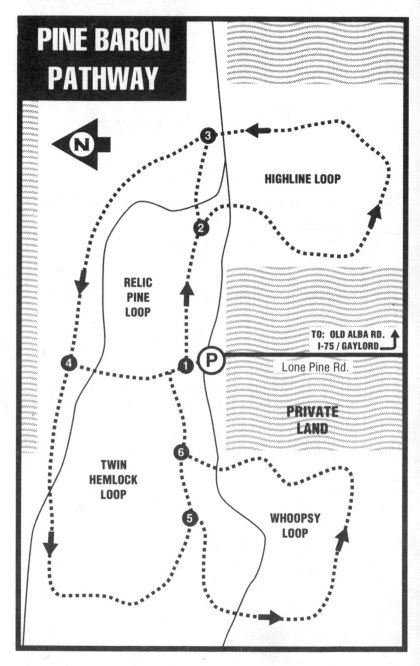

PINE BARON
PATHWAY

N

HIGHLINE LOOP

3

2

RELIC
PINE
LOOP

TO: OLD ALBA RD.
I-75 / GAYLORD

P

Lone Pine Rd.

1

4

PRIVATE
LAND

6

TWIN
HEMLOCK
LOOP

5

WHOOPSY
LOOP

Pine Baron Pathway

County: Otsego
Total Mileage: 6.2 miles
Terrain: Mostly flat land covered with pine and a few hardwoods.
Fees: None
Difficulty: Easy

The appropriately named Pine Baron Pathway is great for beginning riders as well as enjoyable for the more experienced mountain biker. The gently undulating pathway meanders through a beautiful northern Michigan pine forest with a few hardwoods mixed in. As an added bonus, the trees make an excellent wind shield for those frequent blustery days we have during spring and fall.

The nice wide DNR pathway is a popular double-tracked ski trail in the winter. A few of the sections are two-way, but most are one way, making good riding and conversation possible.

The total distance around the outside of all four loops is 6.2 miles. Each loop is a little over 2 miles in length, which is another nice feature. You can add or detract distance as you wish, making it a great family area.

You pass an abandoned homestead along the back section of Twin Hemlock. Just another reminder that our sandy northern Michigan soil makes for poor farming. During the Great Depression in the 1930s a lot of poor, itinerant farmers moved to northern Michigan because of the cheap land available for homesteading. They soon found out it was unsuitable for conventional farming, and most left leaving the buildings as a legacy to that era.

Getting There: From I-75 depart at exit 279 and follow Old Alba Road west for about 3 miles. Turn north on Lone Pine Road and the trailhead is at the end of the road.

Information: Contact the Gaylord DNR District office, P.O. Box 667, Gaylord, MI 49735; ☎ (517) 732-3541.

Pine Baron Pathway

Distance: 6.2 miles
Trail: Double track
Direction: Counter clockwise

From the trailhead head right to reach Post 2 in a half mile. The pathway is extremely well marked with maps at every intersection and signs specifically pointing the way to the parking lot.

The first loop is called the Highline Loop but there aren't any power or high lines along this section. It's just a pleasant 1.2-mile ride through a beautiful pine forest. You arrive at Post 3 at *Mile 1.7* and have the option to head back to the parking lot to complete a 2.5-mile loop.

The next loop is called Relic Pine. This section is also encased in pine trees. It's an easy ride over to Post 4, reached at *Mile 2.6*. Again, you can return to the parking lot in about a half mile by heading left.

Continuing straight takes you around Twin Hemlock, which is the only loop that rolls through a hardwood forest. The trail meanders along the edge of clearing, which was the old homestead. You'll see the weathered buildings through the trees on the right.

After passing over an old farm lane, the pathway swings south to post 5 near **Mile 4**.

By the time you reach the next post the hardwoods have given away to a pine forest again. Continue straight ahead at Post 5 if you want to go back to the parking lot for a 4.4-mile ride. However, you'll miss the most interesting of the four loops.

The Whoopsy loop is the longest single stretch of trail on the pathway. This 1.5-mile section actually has a couple of small dips through a valley that provide a little downhill run and gentle climb up the other side. It's also a very scenic section. The pines are spaced a little further apart and provide small, grassy meadow-like openings. It's only a half-mile to the next post as you swing north after dipping through the small valley for the second time.

When you reach Post 6 at **Mile 5.5**, head right, and you'll soon be back at the parking lot.

As busy as the pathway is in the winter, it doesn't get a lot of use during the summer. You'll probably have the place pretty much to yourself. Enjoy an easy, peaceful ride through a typical northern Michigan pine forest.

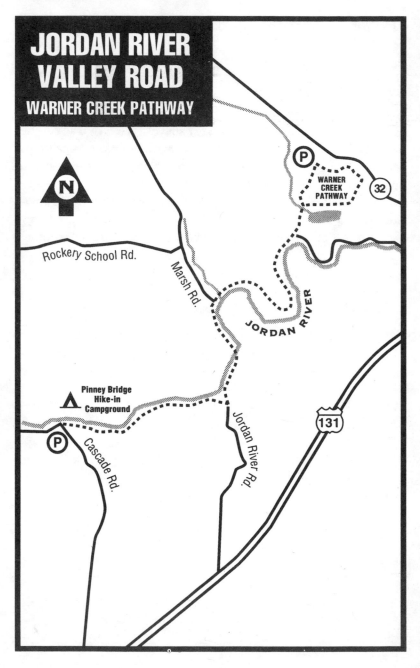

JORDAN RIVER VALLEY ROAD
WARNER CREEK PATHWAY

Warner Creek/Jordan Valley Road

County: Antrim
Total Mileage: 10 miles on a point-to-point route
Terrain: Scenic Jordan River Valley
Fees: None
Difficulty: Easy

This is a great ride through one of Northern Michigan's most scenic river valleys. It actually crosses through two distinctly different valleys separated by a low ridge of hills.

Warner Creek Pathway sits in the first small valley dominated by O'Briens Pond. A short segment of the North Country Trail takes you over to Pinney Bridge Road, which follows the wild, beautiful Jordan River down the valley floor. This is a 10-mile, point-to-point ride or a 20-mile day if you return to the Warner Creek Pathway trailhead along the same route.

Before the ride, stop at Deadman's Hill Overlook, which is just a few miles south of M-32 off US 131. From this high ridge overlooking the valley, the beauty of nature, drama of history and the quiet solitude of the remote northwoods unfold in a spectacular panorama.

The 19th century settlers that settled this land likely scanned the lush valley and river from

these same prominent heights and proclaimed that this must be the river to the promised land...the Jordan.

From the overlook, you're looking at the headwaters of the Jordan. The valley stretches out 400 feet below you. Endless ridges blend into the horizon. On a sunny day, bring a picnic lunch, take your time and enjoy this magnificent view. Occasionally you'll spot eagles riding the thermal currents hovering over the valley.

Deadman's Hill was named when in 1910 a young lumberman lost his life trying to take a team of horses and a load of lumber down the steep slope.

This is the gateway to Michigan's first Natural Scenic River, designated in 1972. It's a piece of Michigan that is primitive, un-settled and still much like it was when settlers first arrived.

The overlook at Deadman's Hill is also the trailhead for the Jordan Valley Pathway, an 18-mile trail that loops through the val-ley and is open to hikers only. Much of the valley floor is quite boggy and wet, the reason mountain bikes are not permitted on the Jordan River Pathway. It's environmentally unsound. Please honor that request, and ride only on the road while in the valley.

Portions of the Warner Creek Pathway can also be wet in the spring so it's wise to do this ride in either summer or fall.

Getting There: The Warner Creek Pathway trailhead is where you start this ride. It's located on M-32 about two miles west of US-131. It's only about five miles from the Deadman's Hill Road and US-131 intersection.

Information: Contact the Gaylord DNR District Headquar-ters, P.O. Box 667, Gaylord, MI 49735; ☎ (517) 732-3541.

Warner Creek/Jordan Valley Road

Distance: 20 miles
Trail: Single track, two-track and forest road
Direction: Counter clockwise on Warner Creek Pathway
From the parking lot head to the right. The pathway follows

The Jordan River as viewed in the valley from from Pinney Bridge Road.

mainly an old two-track for the first mile. You ride only a few hundred yards and the trail swings to the south (left).

For the next mile the pathway meanders along the base of a ridge line. Immediately you cross a large upland meadow. If you do this ride in early summer the meadow will be laden with wildflowers. The pathway drops slightly after crossing the meadow down along the edge of a cedar swamp. The trail can be wet along this section.

In about a half mile you clear the swamp-like area and the terrain starts to open up a little more. As the trees become less dense, a pretty stream and valley appear on the right. It's Warners

Creek, which flows from O'Briens Pond just ahead.

Just past **Mile 1**, the trail forks. The left fork continues on around the Warner Creek Pathway, which is unridable any time of the year. The pathway was developed for cross country skiing. It cuts through an extensive wet area along O'Briens Pond, which never completely drys out. Hiking isn't even good through this section.

The right fork is where the North Country Trail intersects the Warner Creek Pathway. In fact, the two share the pathway for the mile you just completed. Continuing south along the NCT for a mile, you connect with Pinney Bridge Road and the Jordan River Valley.

Just ahead on the NCT you come to the western edge of O'Briens Pond. It's a beautiful spot, where the valley floor opens up in both directions and tall wooded hills flank the sides. The pond stretches out to the east, and Warner Creek flows to the north. You cross the stream on a wide, wooden plank as it flows out of the pond. Just to the right is an extensive beaver dam that controls the flow of water from the pond. This is a great spot to observe wildlife and waterfowl.

The NCT continues south as it follows an old two-track that cuts through a notch in the hills. This is the biggest climb you have on the ride. At **Mile 2.2**, the NCT joins Pinney Bridge Road. Head south on the dirt road for a 10-mile ride through the beautiful Jordan River Valley. The NCT swings away in a short distance and joins the Jordan River Pathway, which is off-limits to mountain bikes. You must stay on the road.

The road may be sandy in spots but there are lots of firm sections as well and overall it isn't bad riding. You can ride any distance you want and return. If you ride up to the Pinney Bridge Campground at the western end of the valley, it's approximately 9 miles.

In just a short distance you cross the headwaters of the Jordan River for the first time. If you ride the entire distance, there will be many places to observe this wild and beautiful river as it gathers strength and volume rushing along the valley floor. By the time it leaves the valley on the western end it's a full fledged river. Here, it resembles a stream.

In less than a mile you'll be able to spot Deadman's Hill Overlook along the tall ridge line to the left far above the valley floor. The road continues to follow the river all the way to the Pinney Bridge Campground. The river is in view most of the way.

When you pass the Jordan River Federal Fish Hatchery on the opposite side of the river, you've gone about halfway to Pinney Bridge. Shortly after passing the fish hatchery, the road climbs a slight grade and parallels the river for the next 4.5 miles...until about a half-mile before reaching the bridge and trail to the campground. It's a pretty area. The river tumbles along on the right side cascading through numerous fallen cedars and little grass islands. Tall wooded hills border the left side of the road.

When you reach the bridge, park your bike and take the time to walk around. This scenic location is a great spot to view the river as it rushes out of the valley on its way to Lake Charlevoix. The Jordan River Pathway also crosses the bridge while the campground is a third of a mile north of the bridge up in the hills.

The clearing where the campground is located was a logging camp in 1915. Sixty men worked and lived here along with the teams of horses used to pull the logs out of the valley. The timber harvested here was mostly hardwoods and hemlock, with white pine making up less than 10 percent of the total volume.

To return, just reverse the ride. It won't be boring on the way back. You'll see different things that you didn't notice on the initial ride through, and this area is so beautiful I don't know how anyone could tire of riding through it.

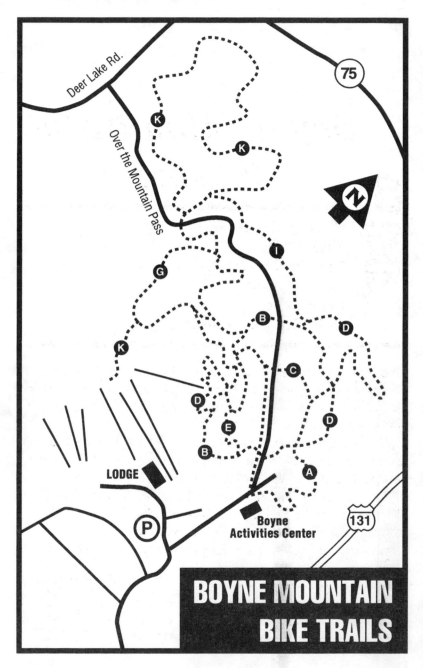

BOYNE MOUNTAIN BIKE TRAILS

Boyne Mountain Resort

County: Charlevoix
Total Mileage: 16 miles
Terrain: Wooded hills surrounding ski area and golf course
Fees: None
Difficulty: Easy to strenuous

Boyne Mountain Resort jumped into the mountain biking arena in 1995 when it opened its extensive Nordican trail system to biking. The trails meander up into the wooded hills that abound on the property.

The bike trails utilize only a portion of the Nordican system. Some of the ski trails traverse the golf course, which mountain bikes obviously can't be allowed on in the summer.

Of the 16-mile system, there are 3 miles that is fairly easy while the rest of the network involves substantial climbs. Most of the trails are wide, designed for two-way traffic. A few are designated one-way in ski season, so I would assume they should be for mountain biking as well.

A portion of the easier trails follow the paved Over The Mountain Pass Road. One possible trip is to simply follow the road to Deer

Lake and back for 3-mile round trip that would feature a good climb in both directions.

The trails start at the Activities Center, near the tennis courts, where maps are available inside. Grab one, you're going to need it. There are no markings on the trails, except for what may be left over from ski season.

Situated in a beautiful valley near Boyne Falls, Boyne Mountain is a full service resort, offering a variety of lodging, an excellent restaurant, health club facilities, and access to several golf courses.

While its sister resort, Boyne Highlands near Harbor Springs, hasn't developed any trails for riding, it might be just a matter of time. Look for big improvements over the next few years in the way of more trails, better signs and possibly even bike rentals.

Getting There: The resort is located just off US-131 about 15 miles south of Petoskey.

Information: For reservations call ☎ (800) GO-BOYNE, or E-mail the resort at *info@boyne.com* or write Boyne Mountain Resort, Boyne Mountain Road, Boyne Falls, MI 49713.

Blue Trail

Distance: 3 miles
Trail: Single and double track
Direction: Counter clockwise

For an easy outing combine the Pancake Trail (Trail A), Blue Trail (Trail B) and Easy Street (Trail C). It's a loop of a little more than 3 miles from the Activities Center. The Pancake Trail begins in a scenic hardwood forest just to the north and winds around the backside of a maintenance compound before linking into Trail C, named Easy Street Trail.

If you want to add another mile of slightly hilly terrain go right on Twister Trail (Trail D) just before you reach Trail C. It's a scenic stretch that winds through a pine studded meadow and by an old abandoned homestead before heading into some low hills forested in hardwoods. Twister eventually joins Blue Trail (Trail B) just before you cross the Over The Mountain Pass Road.

Easy Street (Trail C) merges into the Blue Trail near the old skier's warming hut, which is not used in summer. From here Blue Trail then heads back to the Activities Center trailhead. Along the way Twister Trail (Trail D) splits off to meander a little ways into the low hills around Ramshead chairlift before reconnecting with the Blue Trail and heading back.

The Grinder

Distance: 2 miles
Trail: Single track and access road
Direction: Clockwise

For more challenging terrain and some long, tough climbs, follow Twister Trail (Trail D) and The Grinder (Trail G), which head up the mountain from the Blue Trail (Trail B) for a heart-pounding, 2-mile side trip.

These two trails head uphill together just beyond the warming hut on the return to the trailhead. They immediately begin climbing and basically you don't get much relief until you reach the top after a long and tough ascent.

In a short distance, Trail D takes off to the right and rejoins Trail G as it comes back down the hill, a spot the locals call the "wimp-over." That's because The Grinder makes a another steep climb that doesn't end until you suddenly burst out of the woods near the top. There's an access road at the top, while the first tee for both the Alpine and Monument golf courses looms ahead.

First follow the access road to the left. In a short distance it leads to the top of Boyne Mountain and offers some incredible views of the surrounding countryside, especially in the fall. From the front face, you can also look straight down at the lodge and its famous clock tower. It's beautiful, and worth the climb.

Return along the access road to intersect Trail G again just above the Over The Mountain Pass Road. Watch your speed. It's a fast downhill, as is most of the next mile or so. Either follow The Grinder back down, or cut over to the road and cruise all the way back. It's a 2-mile round trip from the warming hut to the top via The Grinder Trail. Actually Trail G may be a more appropriate designation for this trail, because of the "G" forces you encounter on the downhill run.

Innsbruck Trail

Distance: 5.6 miles
Trail: Single track and double track
Direction: Clockwise

A third option of Blue Trail (Trail B) is to head up Trail I to Innsbruck Trail (Trail H). This would add another 5.6 miles to the ride.

The I Trail, also labeled the Low Road, is just about all climb before it ends at the Innsbruck Trail in 1.24 miles. You also follow it on the return to the Blue Trail and then it's a blast coming back down.

Innsbruck Trail (Trail H) is a real roller coaster ride through a hardwood forest as it is constantly climbing hills, including some long ascents and downhill runs. Remember it's posted as a clock-like, one-way system and should be ridden that way.

Wildwood Hills Pathway

County: Emmet and Cheboygan
Total Mileage: 9.3 miles
Terrain: Rolling wooded hills and open meadows
Fees: None
Difficulty: Easy to moderate

Located in the upland forests along the hilly border of Cheboygan and Emmet Counties, this is a nice riding pathway. It follows primarily abandoned two-tracks with a little single-track thrown in along with a couple of optional hill spurs that can be added or deleted depending on your energy level.

The pathway is located in a vast valley below Gray Hill, the highest point in Emmet County. This hilly region reminds me of a miniature Smoky Mountain setting. Fortunately the pathway is fairly easy riding, and avoids any extreme hill climbs.

It's a scenic trail. Not in the sense of offering panoramic views, but it does capture the essence of northern Michigan. It rolls through hardwood, stands of pine and across open, wildflower-filled grasslands. The pathway briefly follows an old railroad grade, left over from the

179

lumbering era, and skirts an abandoned homestead.

The 11-mile trail system has three loops, the shortest is Loop 1 at 4.5 miles when ridden from the eastern trailhead off US-27. This 8.8-mile ride follows the outside perimeter of the system from the western trailhead on Wildwood Road.

Getting There: From I-75, depart at exit 310 (Indian River) and head west on M-68 and then south on Old US-27 for a couple of miles. Turn west on to Wildwood Road to reach the trailhead and parking area in four miles.

Coming from Petoskey, take Mitchell Road (CR-58) east 9 miles to Wildwood Road. Turn left on Wildwood Road to reach the trailhead in 3 miles. There is an eastern parking lot, but the spur from this side isn't used as much.

Information: The best DNR office for information on this trail is Gaylord District Office, P.O. Box 667, Gaylord, MI 49735; ☎ (517) 732-3541.

Wildwood Hills Pathway

Distance: 8.8 miles
Trail: Two-track and single track
Direction: Clockwise

From the parking lot, the pathway rolls gently away into a stand of pine. There are supposedly a couple of spurs on the way over to post 2, but it looks like the vast majority of riders follow the main pathway.

After crossing Ream Road, a dirt road, the trail immediately begins to climb through another stand of pine. You crest the hill and then begin a nice easy ride through hardwoods to reach Post 2 at *Mile 1*. Take a left at this junction. After a short climb, you get to enjoy a nice long gentle downhill segment all the way to Post 3, reached just before *Mile 2*. This section and the next one south to Post 5 is a series of long, gentle grades that make for great cruising. There's also some interesting interpretive signs

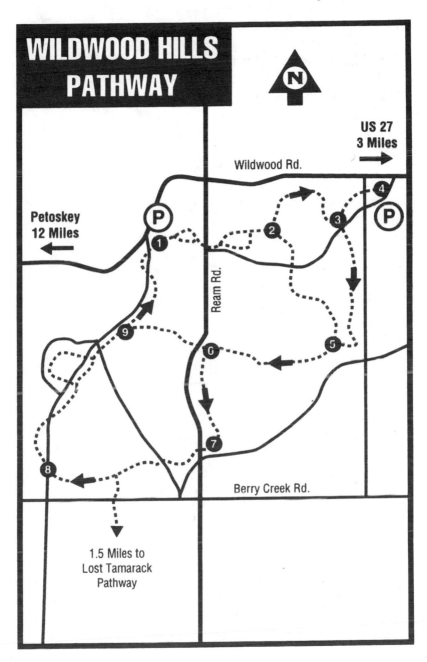

Wildwood Hills Pathway offers the opportunity in many places to either ride single track or follow a dirt road for a more relaxed trip in the Northern Michigan woods.

along this loop. At **Mile 3**, the trail swings sharply right at a "T" intersection after dropping through a pine and maple forest. It's just a third of a mile to Post 5 from the intersection.

The trail continues to wind through a beech-maple forest that is beautiful in the fall. Halfway to Post 6 an interpretive sign points out some bear claws on a tree. After a long but not steep climb, you get to enjoy an equally long downhill run to post 6, reached at **Mile 4.3**.

The mile-long section to Post 7 is a pretty straight forward ride. It starts off with a tough, sandy climb than settles into a roller-coaster ride as it rolls across the hills above the dirt road. You drop down and cross the road at Post 7.

The next 1.4-mile section snakes through forested valleys between tall hills on its way to Post 8. A half mile before you reach the next junction, the trail begins to steadily climb. When you crest the long hill, shortly before reaching Post 8 at **Mile 6.7**, the pathway emerges into a vast meadow filled with wildflowers in the summer. You ride through the meadow for more than a mile.

At Post 8 you can take the dirt road north or follow the single-track trail across the road up into the low hills on the other side. The single track spurs are fun to ride, but they do offer a little challenge. They wind up into the hills and back down, paralleling the dirt road, which is the easier way to travel the 1.3 miles over to Post 9.

This is the section where you pass the crumbling foundation of an old homestead. It's typical of the many little farms that were started and abandoned in early 1900s, when settlers discovered the sandy soil didn't lend itself to productive farming.

At Post 9, reached near **Mile 8**, the trail joins with an old, barely distinguishable railroad bed. This line was used to haul trees to neighboring lumber mills at the turn-of-the-century. You can almost coast the entire 0.75-mile segment back to the parking lot. It's a great finish to the ride.

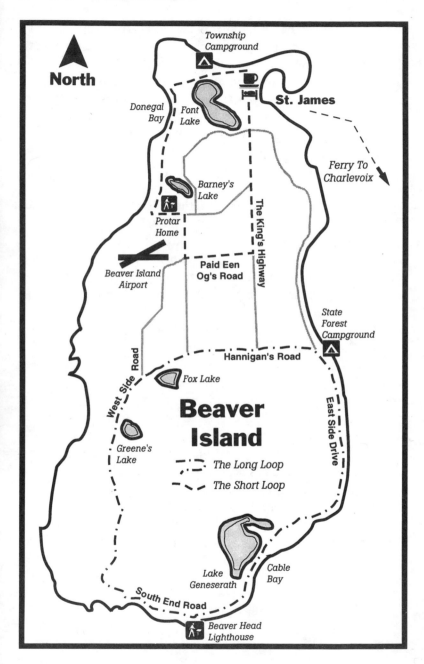

Beaver Island

County: Charlevoix
Total Mileage: 34 miles
Terrain: Large island featuring beautiful sand beaches, forests, marshes, low hills and several inland lakes.
Fees: Round-trip ferry ticket
Difficulty: Easy

From the depths of northeast Lake Michigan, Beaver Island rises 32 miles or a two-and-a-half-hour ferry trip from the docks in Charlevoix. The largest island in Lake Michigan (third largest in the Great Lakes), it's home to 400 year-round residents. Many trace their roots to the 19th century Irish immigrants who made the island a bustling commercial fishing port.

Isolation preserves the beauty and unhurried pace of the 53-square-mile island. In the village of St. James you can stroll the harbor road, relax in the Shamrock pub or hike to windswept Whiskey Point to admire the 19th-century lighthouse. Visitors to the Mormon Print Shop and Museum learn about the island's most notorious historic figure, Mormon leader James Jesse Strang, who proclaimed himself a king. The

185

Mormons were in control of the island from roughly 1840 until 1856 when Strang was assassinated by a couple of his own followers. After his death the Irish settlers once again took control.

During the island's heyday at the turn-of-the-century the population of Beaver was around 2000. Fishing and timber made the island one of the most important ports on the Great Lakes. As the fishing died out and shipping entered the modern era, the population reached a low of 150 in the 1960s. Today tourism and second-home construction have given the island new life.

Mountain bikes are a great way to explore the island. Beyond the immediate area around St. James, there is little pavement on Beaver Island. Many of the roads are graded but those in the southern half of the island can be especially rough. Described here are a 12.5-mile Short Loop and a 21.5-mile Long Loop.

The Short Loop begins in the port of St. James and is an easy ride that explores the more populated northern third of the island. This is where most of the open land of old homesteads are located. You'll pass many old interesting buildings, a few historic sites and a section of newer homes along the western shore of the island that remind you of Cape Cod.

The Long Loop is a circle ride around the south half of the island that can be started from a number of locations, depending on where you are staying.

This is a beautiful ride in the fall. Because of being surrounded by water, fall comes to the island later than the mainland. I've been here as late as the third week of October and found wonderful colors. An added bonus is that there are few tourists that time of year. I had only two cars pass me on the entire ride. Of course, you take your chances with the weather.

Lodging choices on Beaver range from motels and cabins to campgrounds. The St. James Township Park campground on the north end of the island is the closest to the ferry dock and attracts a fair number of mountain bikers throughout the summer. The rustic facility has tables, vault toilets, and a picnic area that overlooks Garden Island to the north. The other facility is a state forest campground located 8 miles south of St. James on East Side Drive.

Getting There: Beaver Island can be reached by air, but the ferry is much more affordable. The boat runs from mid-April to late December and during the summer there are two to three trips a day. You'll need to purchase a round-trip ticket for yourself and another for your bike and should expect to pay around $40. For times and exact ticket prices on the ferry contact the Beaver Island Boat Company at ☎ (616) 547-2311. For flight information contact the Island Airways at ☎ (616) 547-2141 or ☎ (616) 448-2326. Reservations are advised for both forms of transportation, especially during the summer months.

Information: For a list of lodging or other businesses on the island contact Beaver Island Chamber of Commerce, P.O. Box 5, Beaver Island, MI 49782; ☎ (616) 448-2505.

Short Loop

Distance: 12.5 miles
Trail: Dirt roads
Direction: Clockwise

Head south out of town on King's Highway, the only little bit of paved road outside St. James. It doesn't last long before giving way to dirt. Continue riding straight south on King's Highway as it rolls across the countryside, which alternates between cleared and wooded land. A lot of the old homesteads existed along this road. The bottom two-thirds of the island is wooded...sometimes so heavy it forms a canopy over the road.

At **Mile 4**, you come to a "T" intersection with Paid Een Og's Road. Head right. The stone house on the corner is nearly a century old. Across the road, just south of the stone house, is an old wooden fence line that dates to the 1800's. You will find a few more of these scattered around the top third of the island.

Head east on Pain Een Og's Road to the next intersection at

Mile 5.5. The road cuts through more old homestead as the terrain continues to alternate between wooded and cleared.

At Donnel Mor's Lane, go right. It's a mile to the next intersection as you ride by the Beaver Island Airport. Take a left on Sloptown Road at **Mile 6.5**.

Bordered by huge old oak trees and a turn-of-the-century wooden fence, this is a beautiful lane. You pass Bonner Centennial Farm on the left and Protar Home on the right...both historic landmarks. It's 0.7 mile to the next intersection, where you turn right.

The road doesn't have a name but it leads back to Protar's Tomb. where an interesting stone carving of his head adorns the tomb. Before reaching the tomb you'll see a large white cross on the right. It marks the site of an early-century train wreck which took the engineer's life. The next two miles follows the old railroad grade.

Shortly after passing the tomb the road gives way to a trail, which you follow for the next 1.5 miles. This stretch begins with a gentle downhill run that takes you into a beautiful valley. Shortly after reaching the valley floor you ride near the west side of Barney's Lake. Tall sand dunes dominate the northern side of the lake. Take the time to hike up into the dunes. It's very scenic and will provide great views of the lake and valley.

Continuing north on the trail, the next intersection is reached at **Mile 9**. As you continue to roll through the valley, tall wooded hills bordering both sides of the trail form a canopy over the trail. Shortly before reaching the end of the trail you pass through a culvert-like tunnel in the hillside. Just ahead is an intersecting trail and a "modern" home.

Take the time to walk the short distance down to the beach. You're at McCaulley's Point. Looking north you'll swear you're in Cape Cod. This is the modern side of the island, featuring mostly newer homes nestled in the dunescape.

Take your bike out to the right (south of the home). Head left (north) on the dirt road, which cuts through the dunes and Cape-

The Beaver Island Lighthouse, seen on the Long Loop at the south end of the island.

like homes for the next 1.5 miles as you ride along Donegal Bay. After turning left onto the dirt road just before **Mile 10**, needle-like Mt. Pisgah, a prominent dune, rises on your right. It's the highest point on the island.

In a little more than half mile, the road swings right gently climbing out of the dunes on Donegal Bay Road. At **Mile 11.3**, you approach Font Lake, a scenic body of water. After skirting the north end of the small lake, it's 1.3 miles back to St. James. Along the way you pass St. James Township Campground.

Long Loop

Distance: 21.5 miles
Trail: Dirt roads
Direction: Clockwise

This is a circle ride around the south half of the island. Where you stay can dictate where you start this ride. If you stay at the state forest campground, you'll start there. If you stay in St. James and decide to bike down and do the ride, add 16 miles to the above distance.

I like to stay in St. James at one of the quaint motels and rent a wreck to transport the bike and myself to Fox Lake to begin the ride. Old Broncos, that would be considered junk on the mainland, are sustaining a life here as island transportation. Although not pretty, they run and they're cheap. Check with any of the motel proprietors for a rental or reserve one in advance by calling Armstrong Car Rentals at ☎ (616) 448-2513, Beaver Island Jeep at ☎ (616) 448-2200 or Gordon's Auto Clinic at ☎ (616) 448-2438.

Fox Lake is a pretty little inland lake that's located just east of the West Side Road and Hannigan's Road intersection. I like to park along the north end of the lake, a scenic spot to end up after the ride.

Heading east on Hannigan's Road, you come to a major intersection in a half-mile. Follow the road east. It cuts through some deep woods before reaching the intersection with King's Highway at **Mile 2**. Continue straight on Hannigan Road for another until it intersects with East Side Drive at **Mile 3.5**. As you proceed east after the King's Highway intersection, you pass Hannigan's former homestead and orchard on the right.

Right after you swing south on East Side Drive, you come to the entrance to the state forest campground. It's a pretty campground with wooded sites overlooking a beautiful sandy, pristine beach. There's even a pay phone here.

The next 3 miles follows a wide, flat dirt road due south. There are a lot of summer homes here along the shore, but you won't see many of them. The road sits back far enough to limit any lake views along here. As you approach Kitty's Point some lake views open up.

At **Mile 7**, the road swings southwest and cuts back inland away from the lake momentarily. About a half-mile after crossing Cable's Creek the road heads back down along the lakeshore. Lake Geneserath, which you won't see unless you take one of the spurs back, is the largest inland lake on the island.

At **Mile 11**, you pass Kelly's Point, and start your ride along the southern end of the island, a very beautiful section with more views of the lake.

Beaver Island Lighthouse is reached at **Mile 13**. The road rolls through some heavy woods after passing Appleby's Point, the southern most point on the island. The lighthouse is perched on a bluff called Nicksau's Hill and it's open to the public. On a clear day the views of the surrounding smaller islands are impressive. You quickly realize that Beaver Island is the "crown jewel" of a group of islands formed by a glacier that covered North America some 11,000 years ago.

The lighthouse and group of buildings you'll pass as you fly down the hill past Nicksau's Point are home to an alternative educational program for high school students from across the state. They spend the fall semester here and return again in the spring after winter has loosened its icy grip.

For the next half mile you pass through a beautiful dunes area as you round Iron Ore Bay. Just before the road swings away from the bay and up a bluff, pause and walk out on the little jut of land that helps to define the bay. Looking back along the bay, you enjoy a panoramic dunescape scene.

The road now become West Side Road and climbs a series of small hills as it heads inland through a deep forest and heads back north. After cresting Keller's Hill at **Mile 15**, the last climb on the ride, continue straight ahead. I tried taking French Bay Road as an alternative route, but it just disappeared at the edge of a bluff. Island residents say that many side roads end that way. They are still on the map, but haven't been used in decades. You're best staying on main roads through this heavily forested section.

For the next six miles the road meanders through the forest passing Millers Marsh and Greenes Lake on the right. You'll find few clearings along this section of the ride. Most of the island homesteads were built on the north end within walking distance of St. James. Few hardy souls ventured to the southern end. It is quite scenic with the tall hardwoods lining the road. On a hot, sunny day it's normally 10-degrees cooler along this shaded section.

When you reach the next major intersection, West Side Road continues north to the left. Go straight ahead, and you'll be back at Fox Lake in a half mile. Just before reaching the turn-off for Fox, you'll pass a huge boulder sitting on the right. Not native to the island, it was deposited here by the glacier.

North Country Trail

Currently the North Country Trail is open to mountain biking but there is a debate over whether the national trail should be restricted to hikers and backpackers only.

North Country Trail

Is The NCT Open?

When completed the North Country Trail (NCT) will be the longest trail in the country, longer than even the famed Appalachian Trail. From end to end the NCT will be 3,200 miles, extending from the Appalachian Trail in New York to Lake Sakakawea in North Dakota. It will wind through New York, Pennsylvania, Ohio, Minnesota, Wisconsin and North Dakota and Michigan, which has more mileage than any other state at 800-plus miles.

The section that winds through the Manistee National Forest and portions of the Pere Marquette State Forest in the Lower Peninsula has become popular with mountain bikers. There are a number of individual rides that have developed along this section as the firm, mostly single-track trail offers some great riding opportunities.

But be aware that there is some controversy surrounding the use of the trail by mountain bikers. Both the NCT Board of Directors and the National Park Service, which administers some of the funds allocated for trail maintenance, are opposed to mountain bike use on any portion of the trail.

The U.S. Forest Service has the final say for the portion of trail that travels through the national forests, and the Michigan Depected to make a decision sometime in 1996 while the DNR has no plans to ban bikes on any portion of the trail that crosses state forest land.

Before riding any portion of the NCT, check with the appropriate office for the current status of mountain bikers on the particular segment of trail you are interested in. Once on the trail, avoid conflicts with hikers and backpackers by riding in small numbers. If you meet hikers, get off your bike and walk around them. Be courteous at all times. This is not a race course. It's a scenic pathway, and meant to be enjoyed that way. Ride slowly and enjoy the view. It's important that we create a positive image if we want to continue to be able to ride the NCT.

It's also important to remember that the NCT is a point-to-point trail with no designated direction of travel. The major concern of hikers is safety as mountain bikers riding in both directions along a winding single track could result in serious mishaps. Be especially alert around sharp curves, steep slopes and other sections with partially blocked views.

The NCT covers approximately 80 miles between the Timber Creek trailhead on US-10 and Baxter Bridge. It meanders through deep forests, over isolated pockets of hill country and along stretches of scenic bluffs overlooking the Manistee River. Most of it is single-track trail. A few portions follow county roads where state or federal lands give way to private holdings. It's difficult riding at times and isolated except for the road crossings. Most of the NCT is not for the novice or inexperienced rider.

Following are five selected rides along this section of the NCT that offer a circle route utilizing dirt roads and two tracks for the return. If you want to ride out and back on the NCT, however, you can. The trail is marked with either silver diamond-shaped symbols or splotches of blue paint.

Mountain bikers have to remember that the North Country Trail was built for hikers and is a point-to-point trail. Extra caution must be used to avoid serious mishaps between walkers and cyclists.

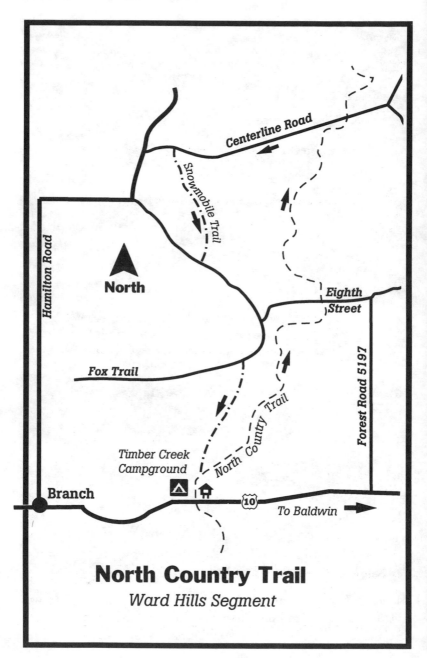

Centerline Road

Snowmobile Trail

North

Hamilton Road

Eighth Street

Fox Trail

Forest Road 5197

North Country Trail

Timber Creek Campground

Branch

10

To Baldwin

North Country Trail
Ward Hills Segment

Ward Hills

County: Lake
Mileage: 12.3 miles
Terrain: Forested hills
Fees: None
Difficulty: Moderate
Trail: Single track and sandy double track
Direction: Counter-clockwise

This 12-mile loop begins at Timber Creek Campground in the Manistee National Forest and heads north into the rugged Ward Hills. It uses a combination of forest roads and snowmobile trails to return to the trailhead from the NCT.

Getting There: This ride begins at the Timber Creek trailhead, which is 7 miles west of M-37 in Baldwin on the north side of US-10.

Information: Contact the Baldwin Ranger District office, 650 North Michigan Ave., Drawer D, Baldwin, MI 49304; ☎ (616) 745-4631.

From the trailhead head north. The first mile is up and down as the trail rolls over low hills through pine forests and heavy undergrowth.

The second mile is through mostly hardwoods. At **Mile 1.5** there is a long climb and after cresting the hill in a quarter mile, you begin a nice downhill run that carries you back into a pine forest at **Mile 2**. A gentle climb of a third of a mile brings you to a pine plateau for another mile of fairly easy riding.

You cross Eighth Street (dirt road) at **Mile 3.2**. Almost immediately you begin a long, steep climb that brings you to the crest of the Ward Hills within a half mile. The next 0.4 mile is an easy ride across the summit offering some nice overlooks to the south. You see the lower hills where you started gaining elevation before the final assault to reach the top.

When you start down it's a quick ride for about for a third of a mile with some sudden turns. For the next half mile the ride again levels out as it rolls across a pine-covered plateau.

Shortly after **Mile 5** you start a mile-long downhill run. It's a fun stretch when ridden under control. The trail drops in a series of stair-step, switch-backs. The final run-out brings you to Centerline Road, a dirt road, at **Mile 6.2**.

Unless you want to begin the long, long climb back to the top of the Ward Hills, head left (west) on Centerline Road. It's 2 miles over to a two-track that serves as a snowmobile trail in the winter. The two-track is sandy in sports but ridable and heads south along a large open area and then across some low hills.

At **Mile 9.6** you intersect Fox Trail, a dirt road, where you head left (southeast). The road drops down a hill and eventually heads due south passing an intersection with Eighth Street. Continue on around Fox Trail as it swings back to the southwest, heading into bottom land along Tank Creek.

At **Mile 10.8** head south on another snowmobile two-track trail bordering the creek and beaver floodings. It's about 1.5 miles of easy riding back to the trailhead along this two-track.

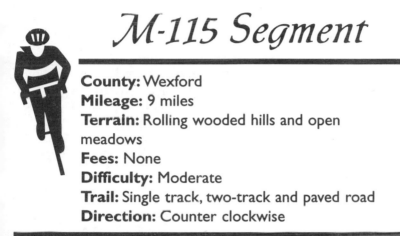

M-115 Segment

County: Wexford
Mileage: 9 miles
Terrain: Rolling wooded hills and open meadows
Fees: None
Difficulty: Moderate
Trail: Single track, two-track and paved road
Direction: Counter clockwise

This is a pretty ride through some upland hills and meadows. It doesn't have the overlooks that the other NCT rides offer, but it also doesn't have the long uphill climbs and the more strenuous terrain. It does require about 3.5 miles of riding along a paved road for the return, or you could opt to ride the trail back. It rides about the same both ways, which is relatively easy for the NCT.

Getting There: From Mesick, head west 3 miles on M-115 to where the trail cuts through a roadside park on the north side of the state highway.

Information: Contact the Cadillac Ranger

District, 1800 West M-55, Cadillac, MI 49601; ☎ (616) 775-8539.

Heading north for the first half mile, the trail rolls through a dense hardwood forest. The next half mile finds the trail dropping down a steep incline where it intersects a faded two-track on the valley floor. Head right, and in a short distance the trail emerges into a long grass-filled valley. The Michigan Northern railroad cuts through the valley. You parallel the tracks for a short distance. Just past **Mile 1** start looking for a blue paint splotch on a log hanging over the trail. It signifies where you should cross the tracks.

Immediately after crossing the tracks, head left. The trail hugs the woodline. Look for a notch in the woods to the right. It's hard to see the paint splotch that marks where the trail re-enters the woods. Roll through a stand of pines and uphill for the next quarter mile.

After reaching the top of the hill at **Mile 1.5**, turn left on a well defined two-track. Follow it for about a half mile and turn right onto another two-track. In a short distance the trail again turns right onto yet another two-track, which rolls through a pine stand. Keep bearing right through the pines. At **Mile 2.8** the trail exits the two-track to the right.

The trail heads sharply downhill crossing an old two-track at the bottom. The trail is not well defined for the next mile. It's one of the newer sections and needs use to establish the pathway. You have to watch carefully for the paint splotches.

The trail meanders up and down three or four partially wooded hills. It alternates between grassland and slightly wooded terrain. It exits onto No. 8 Road, a gravel road, at **Mile 4**.

To return head left on the gravel road for 1.5 miles to paved Harlan Road. Head left (south) and follow Harlan Road 2.5 miles to M-115. It's a mile back east to the rest park on M-115.

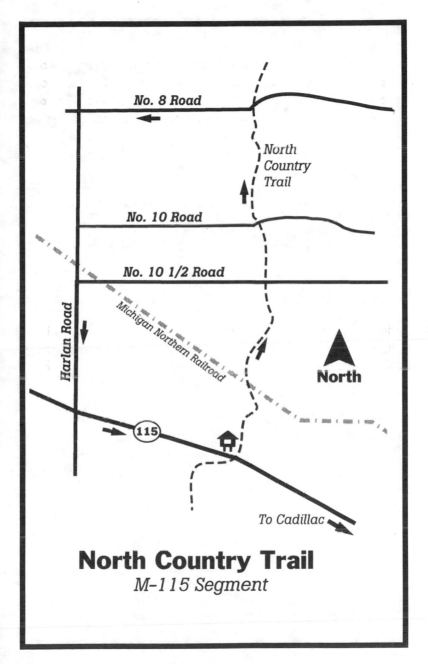

No. 8 Road

North
Country
Trail

No. 10 Road

No. 10 1/2 Road

Harlan Road

Michigan Northern Railroad

North

115

To Cadillac

North Country Trail
M-115 Segment

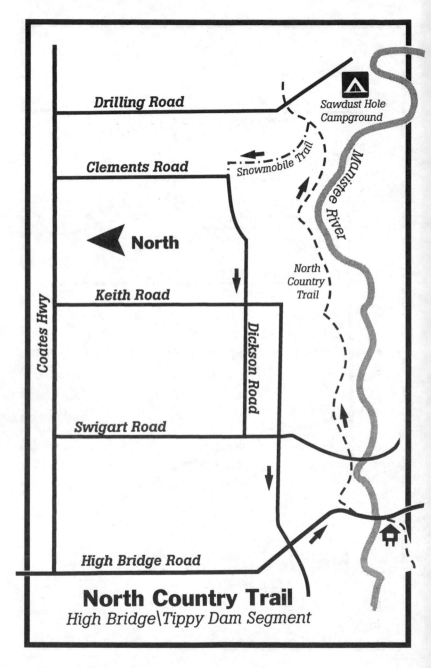

North Country Trail
High Bridge\Tippy Dam Segment

High Bridge-Tippy Dam

County: Manistee
Mileage: 9 mile ride
Terrain: High bluffs and Manistee River valley
Fees: None
Difficulty: Strenuous
Track: Single track and two-track roads
Direction: Counter clockwise

This is one of the most beautiful sections of the North Country Trail in the Lower Peninsula. The trail flows along high, wooded bluffs with beautiful overlooks then plunges down along the valley floor just a few feet above this scenic river.

It's not an easy ride. I wouldn't recommend it for those not used to tight, technical single track and hills. At times the trail is more like a goat path clinging tenaciously to the side of steep hills. There are sections where you have to get off your bike and walk, for both your own safety and the sake of the trail.

Getting There: From Wellston, head west 2.5 miles on M-55 and then north on County Road-669 for 2 miles to High Bridge. You start the ride on the north side of the bridge at the parking area on the west side of the road.

Information: Contact the Manistee District Ranger office, 1658 Manistee Hwy., Manistee, MI 49660; ☎ (616) 732-2211.

The trail starts off by dropping into a low marshy area on the east side of the county road before beginning a steady climb up a wooded ridge. The first couple of miles is narrow and tree-lined as it steadily gains altitude. You cross five wooden bridges, some ridable, some not. Shortly after *Mile 2* the trees give way to a beautiful panoramic view of the Manistee River and the hills on the other side. You're about 300 feet above the valley floor.

The trail descends along more narrow, twisting, tree-lined single-track before quickly dropping onto a two-track at *Mile 2.3*. Watch the hard right turn here.

You're not on the two-track for very long. It quickly turns back into a single track as you head out along a narrow, saddle-back ridge that rises dramatically above the valley. I've often seen deer cavorting in this valley meadow when riding early in the morning. The trail drops down the ridge to a series of steps. Walk your bike here. There are some serious erosion problems along this section, and we don't need to contribute anymore.

After climbing away from the ridge, you ride around the edge of an almost round table top-like, heavily wooded ridge. After skirting the edge of the table top, the trail descends sharply down a series of long switchbacks to a beautiful, long valley and the Manistee River at *Mile 3*. Again, I advise walking your bike down the switchbacks. Riding around the sharp corners without skidding your tires is difficult.

You descend into a 1.5-mile long, crescent shaped valley. The trail quickly reaches the river bank where it meanders along the wide, swift flowing Manistee for a very scenic ride. The open valley is filled with wildflowers in early summer and there are often waterfowl on the river.

The trail crosses a couple of little tributary streams in the valley. The first one is a bit tricky, and I advise walking over the bridge. It occurs at *Mile 3.3*. The second one occurs at *Mile 4.3*, after the trail swings away from the Manistee.

After crossing the second little stream, it's a short distance across an open meadow to the woodline. As you enter the woods, you start a long uphill to the top of the ridge that defines the valley known as "sawdust flats." The trail is steep, narrow and tree-lined.

After reaching the top, take a left on the snowmobile trail which crosses the NCT at *Mile 4.8*. It's a little over a half mile to Dickson Road, a dirt road. Take another left on Dickson Road and follow it for 2 miles to Swigart Road. Turn left again and follow Swigert Road for a short distance to River Road. Turn right on River Road and it's slightly less than a mile over to High Bridge Road. From High Bridge Road it's 0.4 mile back to the parking lot.

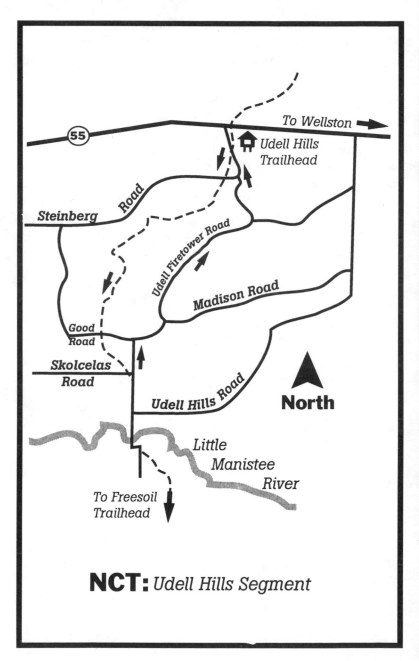

To Wellston

(55)

Udell Hills
Trailhead

Steinberg

Road

Udell Firetower Road

Madison Road

Good
Road

Skolcelas
Road

Udell Hills Road

North

Little
Manistee
River

To Freesoil
Trailhead

NCT: *Udell Hills Segment*

Udell Hills

County: Manistee
Mileage: 11 miles
Terrain: Forested hills and open areas
Fees: None
Difficulty: Moderate
Trail: Firm single track and two-track and dirt roads on the return
Direction: Counter clockwise

The Udell Hills is a small pocket of hills that spring up from a landscape dominated by scoured river valleys. They remind me of a miniature version of the famed Black Hills in South Dakota, minus the monuments.

This portion of the North Country Trail is one of my favorite sections. It's scenic, and very rideable. Some of the climbs are long, but not overly steep. This section even has some mile markers along the trail unlike most portions of the NCT. The trail cuts through the heart of the Udell Hills to offer some nice overlooks.

Getting There: The trailhead is posted on the south side of M-55 in Manistee County, 13.5 miles west of M-37. The nearest community with services is Wellston.

In recent years the amount of bike traffic on the North Country Trail has increased dramatically.

Information: Contact the Manistee District Ranger office, 1658 Manistee Hwy., Manistee, MI 49660; ☎ (616) 732-2211.

The trail immediately crosses the dirt road, which is the return route. The first mile is mostly a flat single track that snakes through the hardwood forest. It begins to climb just before reaching Post Mile 10. The next half mile is a steady climb punctuated by just enough quick dips to keep things interesting.

After crossing a couple of two-track roads on the climb, turn right on the third one at the top of the hill at *Mile 1.4*. Follow it for about a half mile. The trail exits on the right at *Mile 1.9*.

Watch carefully for the trail as it's hard to see. Shortly after the Post Mile 9, you proceed up a short, steep section. At the top is a nice overlook through the foliage just past **Mile 2**.

The next three miles is a single-track delight. It flows along the western ridge of the Udell Hills cascading up and down the ridge flank in gently, rhythmic drops. The trees are tight and the downhills gentle and long. It's an easy way to break into a little technical riding, but watch your speed as you cruise through the trees in slalom-like fashion.

Just before reaching Post Mile 7 at **Mile 5** of the ride, you cross another two-track and start a long climb. After cresting the hill there's a nice overlook to the west. You can see the distant industrial smoke stacks of Manistee, 10 miles to the west.

The last mile drops off the ridge down through a pine stand and dumps you at the corner of Skocelas and Madison roads at **Mile 5.7**.

For the circle ride, head left on Madison and climb the short hill. After initially passing a couple of small homesteads, the dirt road quickly reverts to a scenic two-track. It doesn't even feel like road-riding. In a little over a mile Madison ends at a "T" intersection. Go left on the two-track and follow it to the next "T" at **Mile 8.5**. Head right on Udell Fire Tower Road, and follow it 2.5 miles back to the trailhead.

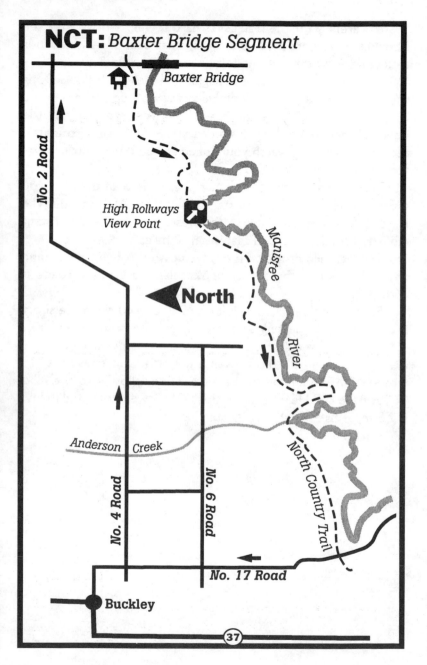

NCT: *Baxter Bridge Segment*

Baxter Bridge

No. 2 Road

High Rollways
View Point

Manistee

River

North

Anderson Creek

No. 4 Road

No. 6 Road

North Country Trail

No. 17 Road

Buckley

37

Baxter Bridge-
Harvey Bridge

County: Wexford
Mileage: 23.5 miles
Terrain: Manistee River bluffs
Fees: None
Difficulty: Strenuous
Trail: Single track and county roads
Direction: Clockwise

This is one of the most scenic rides along the NCT. From high bluffs, it offers more overlooks of the Manistee River valley than any other section along the trail. It's also one of the more rugged rides. I recommend this ride for strong riders only. Please no beginners.

The trail is in relatively good shape, but it does have several steep climbs and descents. Ride these areas under control to minimize erosion. This is one of the sections that the northern chapter of the MMBA has adopted for maintenance. This is the only ride, of those recommended, that traverses state land. It's part of the Pere Marquette State Forest.

Getting There: Begin the ride where the trail crosses County Road-29 1/2 just north of Baxter Bridge. Just east of Kingsley on M-113,

213

you head south on Summit City Road for five miles and then west on County Line Road. Within a half mile turn south on County Road-29 1/2. This is a loop ride and you return on mostly dirt county roads. You could spot a car near Harvey Bridge but the return ride along the county roads is not nearly as hard as the NCT.

Information: Contact the Cadillac DNR District office, 8015 Mackinaw Trail, Cadillac, MI 49601; ☎ (616) 775-9727.

The ride begins on the west side of the road. The first couple of miles involves some of the longest and hardest climbs as you scale the high bluffs above the river valley. Shortly after *Mile 2*, you come to an incredible overlook locally known as High Rollways. It's also accessible by two-track roads, making it a popular picnic spot with locals. This is a great spot to pause and enjoy the view and you'll be ready after the long climb to get here.

At *Mile 3* you drop down a short distance and cross a two-track, one of many you'll cross on the ride. Watch carefully for the trail as you cross through a pine stand. It's challenging to follow the blue paint splotches through here.

After crossing through the pines, the trail heads south for a short distance and swings back out along the bluffs. For the next couple of miles it's one overlook after another. You'll have trouble maintaining a constant pace through this section because of the scenic views.

Between *Mile 5* and *Mile 7*, the trail crosses several rivulets. Some are fairly big as the trail dips down and climbs back up the other side and it's a workout. Views are limited through this section. Shortly after *Mile 7* the trail drops down along the edge of the river for a couple of miles of fairly easy and scenic riding. It's the only time you'll be right along the river.

At *Mile 9.5* you cross swift, flowing Anderson Creek just before it spills into the Manistee, another pretty spot. Right after crossing the creek the trail climbs back up along the bluffs and stays there until you exit onto County Road-17 above Harvey Bridge. At **Mile 11** you pass a monument marking an old Indian trail that ran from near Cadillac and Lake Mitchell to Traverse City and Grand Traverse Bay. You can still see evidence of the trail as it proceeds north.

Once you reach County Road-17 at **Mile 12**, head north 3 miles to County Road-4. Follow it east for 4 miles where it swings north and becomes County Line Road in a little over a mile. County Line Road swings back east and you follow it to County Road-29 1/2, reached in 1.5 miles. Turn south on County Road-29 1/2 and it's slightly less than a mile to where the trail crosses the road.

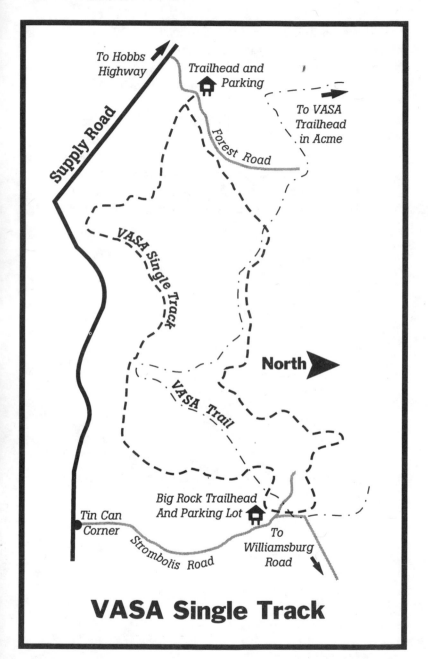

To Hobbs Highway

Trailhead and Parking

To VASA Trailhead in Acme

Supply Road

Forest Road

VASA Single Track

North

VASA Trail

Big Rock Trailhead And Parking Lot

Tin Can Corner

Strombolis Road

To Williamsburg Road

VASA Single Track

Other Trails

VASA Single Track

The Michigan Department of Natural Resources has recently given the go-ahead on a new 14-mile, single-track loop that will crisscross portions of the VASA trail. It will be a separate trail system from the VASA with its own trailhead, although you will be able to access the single-track from the VASA Pathway.

The single track has been in the works for a couple of years. It ties together a series of former ORV trails that were closed to dirt bikes. The project seemed doomed when the DNR announced in the summer of 1995 that they weren't opening any new trail systems until further notice. Because the trails were already in place and many local mountain bikers were already riding the proposed system, the DNR reversed its decision and are permitting the signing of the trail. The VASA Single Track should be ready for use in 1996.

I have ridden many portions of the proposed system and it will be a beauty. Similar to the VASA Pathway in terrain, the Single Track will feature rolling hills, small pristine lakes and heavy forests.

The new system is tight and technical at times, but a great ride. Because of the hilly terrain and more technical nature of the single track, it will be a somewhat strenuous ride. I wouldn't recommend it for beginners.

One of the proposed trailheads will be near the "Big Rock" on Strombolis Road, a dirt road which heads north from Supply Road at Tin Can Corner. Strombolis Road parallels the back part of the VASA Single Track. It's a little more than a mile back to Big Rock from Supply Road. The second trailhead is slated to be just off Supply Road about a half mile beyond the Hobbs Highway intersection.

Big M

Scheduled to open in 1996 is a 46-mile mountain bike trail being developed around the Big M Cross Country Ski Trail by the U.S. Forest Service. The terrain will be much like that of the Udell Hills area of the North Country Trail. A good portion of the new trail system parallels the NCT through the hill country and will provide similar scenic overlooks from the higher elevations.

It will be a long loop ride with a couple of shorter options. The trailhead will be at the Big M parking lot, which is on Udell Hills Road, 3 miles south of M-55 and just west of Wellston.

This single-track trail system will be a huge addition to mountain biking in Michigan as we have few circle loops that come close to this kind of mileage in the Lower Peninsula.

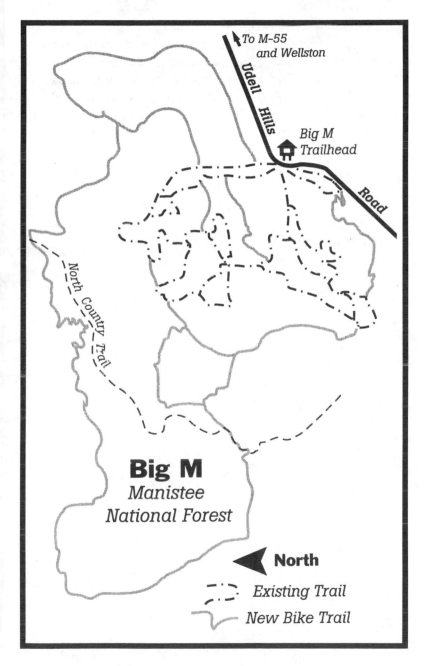

Big M
Manistee
National Forest

North

North Country Trail

To M-55
and Wellston

Udell Hills

Big M
Trailhead

Road

Existing Trail

New Bike Trail

About The Author

Mike Terrell, a Midwestern native, grew up in Indiana, and has since lived in Ohio, Wisconsin, Illinois and Michigan. He and his family reside in the northwestern corner of the Lower Peninsula near Traverse City.

Upon graduating from Florida Southern College with a degree in journalism, he entered the corporate world accepting a position in the public relations department at Firestone. After 13 years of writing news releases about golf, racing and tires (probably in that order), he and his family opted to chuck corporate life, ties and suits for Michigan's northwoods and flannel shirts. (Well maybe Traverse City isn't exactly the northwoods, but it's just out the back door.)

Following his passion for the outdoors, Mike turned to freelance writing doing articles on skiing, biking, canoeing, hiking and travel features. Over the years he has contributed articles on regular basis to Booth Newspapers of Michigan, Chicago Tribune, Minneapolis Tribune, Snow Country and Cross Country Skier. He's the Midwestern Editor for Skiing, the ski and biking columnist for the Traverse City Record Eagle and a contributing editor to the Great Lakes Skier.

In 1995 he authored his first book, Northern Michigan's Best Cross Country Ski Trails in the Lower Peninsula, which is now in its second printing. He is currently at work on a companion book for the Upper Peninsula.

Mike travels throughout the Great Lakes researching articles for skiing and biking. He has written about ski resorts and bike trails along the Niagaran Escarpment overlooking Lake Huron's Georgian Bay, the Canadian Shield wilderness above Sault Ste. Marie, the Sawtooth Mountains overlooking the Arrowhead Region of Minnesota, the fabled Gunflint Trail in the Boundary Waters and Thunder Bay perched on the Lake Superior's northshore. He's traveled extensively throughout Wisconsin and the Black Hills of South Dakota.

PUBLICATIONS

Bicycling books from Pegg Legg Publications

Cycling Michigan: *The Best 25 Bicycle Routes In Western Michigan,* By Karen Gentry

Cycling Michigan: *The Best 30 Bicycle Routes In East Michigan,* By Karen Gentry

Mountain Biking Michigan: *The Best Trails In Southern Lower Michigan,* By Dwain Abramowski and Sandra Davison

Mountain Biking Michigan: *The Best Trails In Northern Lower Michigan,* By Mike Terrell